WELCOMING THE
CHILDREN

EXPERIENTIAL
CHILDREN'S
SERMONS

BRANT D. BAKER

Augsburg
MINNEAPOLIS

WELCOMING THE CHILDREN
Experiential Children's Sermons

Scripture quotations are from the New Revised Standard Version Bible, copyright © 1989, Division of Christian Education of the National Council of the Churches of Christ in the United States of America.

Cover design by David Meyer
Interior design by Northwestern Printcrafters
Interior art by RKB Studio

Library of Congress Cataloging-in-Publication Data

Baker, Brant D., 1958–
    Welcoming the children: experiential children's sermons /
  Brant D. Baker.
      p. cm.
   ISBN 0-8066-2835-9 (alk. paper)
   1. Children's sermons.   2. Worship (Religious education)
I. Title.
BV4315.B255   1995
252'.53—dc20
                                        95-22318
                                             CIP

Manufactured in the U.S.A.   AF 9-2835
99 98 97 96 95 1 2 3 4 5 6 7 8 9 10

*This book is dedicated
to all the children of
Providence Presbyterian Church,
and especially
to Kellen and Gray*

CONTENTS

Contents

INTRODUCTION

What Experience Has Taught Us

For years I have met for premarital counseling with couples asking to be wed. One of the topics discussed was child rearing, especially the challenges of raising two or more children. My usual line, gleaned from some long forgotten source, was, "Two children is not twice as hard as one, it is four times as hard."

This sage advice was happily dispensed through the first decade of my ministry. Then something happened: My wife and I had our second child. The usual challenge of long nights was made more challenging by even longer days as we tried to keep up with the two-year-old demands of our first child in between the colic cries of our second.

And suddenly I knew, in a way I had never known before, that the sage advice was true. Experience had created an opportunity for knowing the truth in a way that went far beyond words.

Experience continues to be the most promising method of conveying truth to children, as well. The children's sermons offered in this collection follow the experiential method outlined in my earlier book, *Let the Children Come*. This method proposes that children learn best not by hearing, not by seeing, but by *doing*. For children, as well as for pastors-become-parents, experience communicates the truth of our life and faith more deeply, more loudly, and more meaningfully than words.

This importance of experience is recognized by the church at many levels. We provide a tangible liturgy (standing, sitting, singing, saying); we seek to involve people in "hands-on" kinds of ministries, knowing that these will fire hearts in ways no special mission offering ever can; and we hold a high view of the sacraments, which are themselves the ultimate experience of God's holy, transcendent mystery.

When it comes to more traditional forms of education, however, we somehow lose sight of our experiential intuition. In Sunday school, we often rely on heavily word-oriented forms of teaching, with perhaps some arts and crafts thrown in if we are dealing with younger students. What is true of Sunday school is absolutely true of sermons, so much so that our culture dismisses the notion of "sermon" as a ponderous, one-sided bombardment of words.

What Incarnation Has Taught Us

Any effort to communicate our faith must incorporate a fundamental truth of Christianity: that Jesus Christ came and dwelt among us, that we might *experience* the fullness of his grace and truth. Experience and incarnation are linked inextricably and inexplicably: it is God's grace and design for life that we learn truth through an encounter (experience) with God enfleshed (incarnate).

To talk about an experience of incarnation is to talk about *relationship*. The model set by our Lord is to be played out in the church, namely, that we enter into relationships with one another in order to learn something of God. As we have seen and heard from Christ, so we are to do.

Two key aspects of this basis for educational ministry involve a willingness to risk revealing ourselves and a willingness to take seriously the mutuality of ministry. Risk may mean that as we offer a children's sermon, we give up the formal distance that separates us from the children. It may mean that, as leaders, we risk entering into the playful world of children by becoming more childlike ourselves. In so doing, we build bridges to communicate the deeper truths of the Gospel.

The second aspect of an experiential practice of Christian education is mutuality of ministry. Those of us who offer children's sermons must be open to the possibility that we might learn something from the children we teach. We become partners in the educational exchange by welcoming the transcendental moments afforded by education with children in general and children's sermons in particular.

What the Developmentalists Have Taught Us

In my earlier book, *Let the Children Come*, I reviewed the developmental basis for an experiential approach to the children's sermon. If we take seriously the insights of child development experts such as Jean Piaget, we should not expect children ages two through ten to make analogical jumps—*this* is like *that*—the teaching basis behind almost all object lessons. *But* children of this age are very capable of making imaginative jumps. And their ability to see the imaginary opens up a whole world of possibilities within the confines of the sanctuary walls.

The work of Erik Erikson regarding psychosocial development in children teaches us that we should not expect our young audience to sit perfectly quiet and still while we preach at them. Children ages two through ten are curious and eager to explore, to wiggle, to use their bodies in expressive ways, and to investigate new worlds. They are also very open to working together to co-create, to be truly involved in a mutual ministry of making a sermon happen.

In her book, *Sharing Faith with Children*, Sara Juengst offers the following helpful insights on children ages two to six:

They are egocentric.
They are unable to think abstractly.
They are confused by symbolism.
They are curious.
They live in a world of imagination and fantasy.
They are best taught concepts by example.
They have a limited understanding of personality.
They crave acceptance and affection.
Their horizons are expanding.
Their reasoning ability is developing.
They still have a limited concept of time.
They are assimilating and accommodating information.[1]

Juengst's insights support the use of methods beyond the object lessons and moralisms all too often found in children's sermons. She distinguishes between the experiential sermon model and a storytelling model, which she suggests is probably the best way to preach to a young audience. What seems even better to me, however, is storytelling with enough experiential handles to engage children completely. It is this kind of storytelling that I am calling *experiential Christianity*.

Building on What We Know—Toward Transcendence
The gospel is full of surprising twists and turns, things that upset our usual way of seeing things. Children's sermons offer an opportunity to experience this same sense of disequilibrium through

a "discrepant event," something that goes in a way no one (per-haps not even the leader!) expects.

Such events signal a special receptor in our brain. This receptor is in the business of helping our brain know which events to pay attention to and which to ignore. Events that create disequilibrium get the attention of this receptor and tell it to pay attention. What educators call the "teachable moment" has arrived.

Such discrepant events also have a theological impact: They can at times signal a brush with transcendence. To be human is, in large part, to know that there is "something more." We seek an encounter with the Other, a moment when we go beyond our limits and limitations to experience the wonder and awe of the Living God. Moments of disequilibrium—discrepant events—can startle us into heightened receptivity and open the way for a new understanding and awareness of God.

Such moments put us off balance when they do come. For de-spite our yearning, they either catch us off guard, or overwhelm our reality, or both. In either case, they certainly get our attention. Children's sermons often frighten us because there is so much room for unscripted, nonliturgical, *discrepant* events to happen. But it is precisely this *unstructured* aspect of children's sermons that makes them ripe with transcendental expectation and possi-bility.

As we welcome children into a relationship of mutual ministry, we become more and more aware that our experiences together bring us to the threshold of a discrepant event that will grip our hearts in new and deeper ways.

What We Have Learned about the Creative Process
Despite all our talk about experiential teaching methods and the-ology of incarnation, despite all our worshipful expectation of a brush with transcendence, our children's sermons easily can be undone if we lose one most basic insight: The children's sermon is a *sermon*, complete with all the preconditions, preparations, and challenges.

If nothing else, the creative process behind a sermon presumes a text. The Word of God is the holy history of God's covenantal grace, it is the guide for sanctified living, and it is a wonderful cor-rective for the vague, trite, moralistic, and otherwise misleading "texts" that children's sermons are often built on. It is fairly easy to start a children's sermon with the story of what happened to me when I went out to work in the garden, or when I got a flat tire, or when our dog ate our little girl's favorite toy (and don't worry about the scripture text; after all, we can wait to read that after the children are dismissed). It is much more difficult to wrestle with the Word of God, to dwell with a text long enough to learn a fitting method for its communication. (And, it also may be difficult to rearrange the order of service so that the text is read before the Word is preached!)

All of this is to say that the creative process does not begin in a vacuum. It must begin with God's Word. Preachers know that an adult sermon must be based on a text from Scripture. The latest movie, a novel we've just read, a funny thing that happened on the way to the men's fish dinner—any of these may illustrate; but if they become the text, we have missed the point and our calling. In the same way, the children's sermon *must* be drawn from scripture text. Anything else is pretext.

I was recently working on a children's sermon, trying to get it out of the way so I could turn my attention to the "adult sermon." The text was the first two verses of Romans 12, especially the second verse, "do not be conformed . . . but be transformed . . . " I suddenly realized, as I struggled to put these concepts into experiential form, that I hadn't done the exegetical work needed to understand what Paul meant by "transformed." I began doing some word searches and learned that the word Paul used in Romans 12:2 is also used in Matthew and Mark, but is translated "transfiguration." This was getting interesting.

Further research showed that the Greek word for both "transformation" and "transfiguration" is "metamorphosis." From there the ideas began to blossom. Rather than dealing with something abstract (transformation), I could use a concrete example of an organic change that occurs in nature. The resulting children's sermon, "Rocks and Flowers," was a wonderful experience for children *and* adults.

Once the beginning point for the creative process has been firmly established, the next step is taking time to dream the question, "If we could do anything to experience this topic or text—*anything*—what would we do?" For me this dreaming becomes a prayerful exercise that cannot be rushed or forced. (In fact, I've noticed that the less time I've allowed for sermon preparation, the less inspired the final outcome is likely to be.) In the "Rocks and Flowers" sermon mentioned above, the question was "If we could do anything to communicate experientially the concepts of conforming and transforming, what would it be?" My word study had unearthed the organic imagery of a metamorphosis for the idea of "transforming." From there it was only a short creative leap to another organic image to communicate "conforming," an image of the pressure felt by a rock.

The next step in the creative process is assessing the resources on hand and modifying our dream to that reality. I always look to the congregation as a major resource and work hard to include them in some way. In addition to the good theology of welcoming the adults to move from observers ("Isn't that cute?") to partici- pants (ripe with transcendent potential), getting everyone in- volved is just good, plain *fun*.

And last, but certainly not least, we must never forget that the Holy Spirit is alive and well in the creative process. In fact, when we search for ways to "inspire" our listeners, when we pray and wait for inspiration, we are acknowledging the most important stage of the creative process. To say we are inspired is a faith claim about the role of God's Spirit in creativity. The Greeks un- derstood "ideas" as supernatural insights arrived at through the spirit. When we have a creative idea, it seems very much the case that God's Spirit is at work within us. And when we take the time prayerfully to seek God's Spirit, we are intentionally opening our- selves to a creative power far greater than our own.

About Using This Book

The suggestions and thoughts in the following pages should be seen as outlines to be enfleshed in you and the children in your congregation. Any attempt to transplant these sermons verbatim will not only come across as stiff, but will also deny the sponta- neity, creativity, and fun that lurk in any communication event. It is better to phrase the sermons in your own words, to tailor them to your audience and setting, and to allow for improvising after responses from the listeners. More will happen to surprise both you and the children if you feel comfortable and relaxed enough to let serendipity play a part.

One thing that can prevent a wholesale transplant of these sermons is the difference of physical resources. As you will see, "church geography" plays an important role in a number of the events. Use what you have. If you have two outside aisles and a smaller church, you've got a great place to "march around Jericho" seven times. If you have a balcony, why not go up there for a series of sermons "on mountaintops" (Noah, Abraham, Moses, Jesus)? The potential you find in your own church geography will depend on how carefully and how creatively you study it.

Two suggestions from my previous book bear repeating as you plan children's sermons. First, be sure you have a plan—a firm, clear idea of where you're going and what you want to do with your sermon. Second, have sense of humor, a willingness to laugh with the children and at yourself.

Work with your congregation to help them want to participate. Unless you are blessed with an extremely flexible group, it may take a few months of using these kinds of children's sermons before the congregation realizes that they are welcomed, and in some cases expected, to participate. A note in the bulletin about what you are going to ask of them can be a big help if they are new at this kind of thing. You might also start with sermons that you feel would be less "threatening" to your congregation. Building trust for making unusual requests and learning how to communicate unusual ideas to large groups of people both take time.

Finally, explore your own creativity. Since the children's sermon is necessarily tied to a biblical text, theexamples in this collection may or may not fit the preaching plan on any given Sunday. Adjust. Adapt. Expand. Improvise.

My prayer is that you will use these examples as jump-off points for exciting, creative, and dynamic children's sermons of your own—ones that can trigger new understandings and experiences of transcendence in yourself as well as in all your listeners.

God bless your efforts!

BIBLE STORIES

WHEN GOD ROCKS THE BOAT (Noah's Ark)

Scripture: Genesis 6:11-22; 7:6-10; 8:1-5, 20-22
Focus: The church is a unique place in its safety from life's storms, a sanctuary in which to come together under God's protection when the waves threaten to wash over us.
Experience: To come into the church two by two, like the animals coming into Noah's ark.
Arrangements: None are needed, but if you have a small congregation you might choose to involve everyone by asking the congregation to move into the narthex as you begin the children's sermon, or to line up at side aisle doors (if available) to be ready to loop back through the narthex in pairs.

LEADER: Good morning! Do you think it looks like rain today?

CHILDREN: No!

L: No, and I'll bet it didn't look like rain when Noah started work on the ark. (Or, if yes, "I'll bet it looked a lot like it does today when Noah finished work on the ark.") What was the ark for?

C: To keep Noah's family and the animals safe.

L: Right. God had Noah take his family and the animals inside to keep them safe. And the animals went into the ark two by two. (*Discuss as much about the flood story as you think necessary for your particular group of children; then:*) Did you know that the church is the same kind of safe place as the ark? In fact, let's go back to the narthex and come in two by two just like the animals went into the ark—you can even pretend to be an animal if you want—and that way we'll remember that this church is a lot like Noah's ark, a safe place where we can be protected by God. (*Children, and congregation if appropriate, meet in the narthex and come in as animals. You may want to provide commentary about the number of elephants and monkeys there seem to be in this church, etc.*)

L: Let's have a prayer of thanks for this place of safety and God's protection. (*Prayer.*)

ABRAHAM JAM (*The Promise of Isaac*)

Scripture: Genesis 12:1-9 (and other stories from the Abraham cycle)
Focus: To fully appreciate our Christian faith, we need to understand something of our Jewish heritage. The focus of this sermon is on Abraham, the "founding father" of Judaism and of the Old Covenant.
Experience: To be involved in a Bible "rap" about Abraham.
Arrangements: You will need to have worked out for yourself the rhythm of the rap (feel free to change it to make it work for you) and be comfortable with the basic flow of the words (memorizing it is probably not necessary). Make a "jam button" for each of the children (construction paper circles lettered with "Abraham Jam Club" with a piece of rolled tape on the back), and perhaps a few larger signs that read "Abraham Jam Club." Sunglasses and other "rapper attire" optional!

Beat for "Abraham Jam"

LEADER: Good morning! Hope you are doing well today. I'd like for you to name some of the famous people in the Bible.

CHILDREN: Jesus.

L: That's right, Jesus is in the Bible. Who else?

C: Matthew.

L: Good. Anyone else?

C: Michael.

L: Uh, maybe so. . . . Anyone else?

C: Bartholomew.

L: Well, that's a pretty good list, but you know what? No one mentioned Abraham! Abraham was one of the most important people in the Old Testament. And since we're learning about him today in worship, let's start a fan club, and call it the "Abraham Jam Club." (*Pass out buttons and signs.*) In fact, I've even got a kind of rap to help us learn a little about Abraham. What we all need to do (*include the whole congregation if you choose*) is to set up a soft beat by saying the words "Abraham Jam, Ya! Abraham Jam, Ya! Abraham Jam, Ya!"

c: "Abraham Jam, Ya! Abraham Jam, Ya! Abraham Jam, Ya!"

L: Good. Say it softly, and keep it going, and I'll try to do this rap
(*put on sunglasses*):

> If you want to know who's who,
>> Abraham's the one for you.
>
> Abraham was one cool dude:
>> he talked to God and was not rude.
>
> God made an oath and Abe had faith;
>> he knew with God he'd be real safe.
>
> Of all bro's in the Bible,
>> Abraham is without rival.
>
> But old Abe thought it was funny
>> when God said he would have a son, he
>
> fell on his face and gave a laugh.
>> He got real lucky, God showed no wrath.
>
> Later Sarah heard the news;
>> she laughed like Abe, shook in her shoes!
>
> But God's the one who had a smile,
>> 'cause a boy was born in a little while.
>
> They called him "Isaac," it means "he laughs."
>> Don't you know his folks will remember that!

(*Prayer*)

A FEW FAITHFUL CHILDREN OF GOD
(*Abraham Pleads for Sodom*)

Scripture: Genesis 18:16-33
Focus: Our God is a God of grace and mercy as much as or more
than a God of judgment and destruction. A second focus is on the
value of even relatively few faithful children of God.
Experience: To act out Abraham's bargaining with God, substituting
members of the congregation for the people of Sodom in the
"numbers game" Abraham played with God.
Arrangements: You'll need an adult or liturgist to give the responses
of God, and a Bible (or abbreviated script) with the dialogue. You
might want to explain to the children that Abraham's response to
God, "Far be it from you, O Lord" (which they will repeat), means,
"You would never do such a thing, O Lord." You may also want to
give some thought to how many pews, sections, etc., comprise about
ten percent of those present during worship in order to instruct that
number to be seated each time the text calls for it.

LEADER: Good morning! Let's meet in the middle of the church today, and let's ask the entire congregation, if they would, to please stand. Today we're going to be part of a Bible story where Abraham bargains with God about how many faithful people it would take for God not to destroy a city. The liturgist will read the part of God, I'll read the part for Abraham, and children, every time I give you the signal, I want you to say part of what Abraham said to God: "Far be it from you, O Lord." *Remember that Abraham means, "You would never do such a thing, O Lord."* Let's practice: When I raise my hand, that will be your cue, and you will say . . .

CHILDREN: Far be it from you, O Lord.

L: Great! Now congregation, watch me so you'll know when you've been auctioned off, so to speak, and can sit down. Everybody ready! OK, the Bible says that God came to visit Abraham and told him that God was going to destroy an evil city called Sodom. Then Abraham said, "Will you indeed sweep away the righteous with the wicked? Suppose there are fifty righteous within the city; will you then sweep away the place and not forgive it for the fifty righteous who are in it?" (*Cue children.*)

C: Far be it from you, O Lord.

LITURGIST: If I find at Sodom fifty righteous in the city, I will forgive the whole place for their sake.

L: Let me take it upon myself to speak to the Lord, I who am but dust and ashes. Suppose five of the fifty righteous are lacking? (*Motion to about one-tenth of the congregation to be seated.*) Will you destroy the whole city for lack of five? (*Cue children.*)

C: Far be it from you, O Lord.

LIT: I will not destroy it if I find forty-five there.

L: Suppose forty are found there. (*Motion for another tenth of congregation to sit. Cue children.*)

C: Far be it from you, O Lord.

LIT: For the sake of forty I will not do it.

L: Oh do not let the Lord be angry if I speak. Suppose thirty are found there. (*Motion for another tenth of congregation to sit. Cue children.*)

C: Far be it from you, O Lord.

LIT: I will not do it if I find thirty there.

L: Let me take it upon myself to speak to the Lord. Suppose twenty are found there. (*Motion for another two-tenths of the congregation to be seated. Cue children.*)

C: Far be it from you, O Lord.

L: For the sake of twenty I will not destroy it.

LIT: Oh do not let the Lord be angry if I speak just once more. Suppose ten are found there. (*Motion for remainder of congregation to be seated so that only children remain standing. Cue children.*)

C: Far be it from you, O Lord.

LIT: For the sake of ten I will not destroy it.

L: And the LORD went his way, when he had finished speaking to Abraham; and Abraham returned to his place. Let's have a prayer and thank God that even as few as we are, if we are faithful, we can save a city! (*Prayer.*)

WHAT'S IN A NAME?
(*The Meaning of Jacob's Name*)

Scripture: Genesis 25:21-26
Focus: As Christians, we are confronted with an important choice: Do we spend our lives grabbing all we can in order to get ahead (as we are often taught to do by society), or do we grab hold of the protection and blessings that God offers us?
Experience: To grab one another's heels, as Jacob grabbed Esau's at birth; and then to grab for God, as we hear the various meanings of Jacob's name.
Arrangements: None are needed.

LEADER: Good morning! We need to stand in a circle. (*You may need more than one circle if your group is larger than your space, or else meet in the aisle and make a line instead.*) That's great! Now, stoop down and grab the heel of person standing to your right (in front of you). Everybody got it?

CHILDREN: (*With laughter and grunts!*) Yes!

L: Great! Now I want to tell you a story—don't let go of those heels—a story about the twin brothers Jacob and Esau. When they were being born, Jacob grabbed Esau's heel. In fact, that's one way to translate Jacob's name: In Hebrew, the name Jacob can mean "he grabs by the heel." Why do you suppose Jacob was holding Esau's heel?

C: I don't know. So he wouldn't fall. To hold him back.

L: The Bible story makes it sound as if Jacob were trying to hold Esau back, as if Jacob were trying to get ahead of Esau so that he could be the first born. Well, we've been holding each other's heels for a few minutes now. Does anybody feel that they're getting ahead of anyone else?

C: No!

L: Okay, you can let go, and while we're standing up straight, let me read you the first verse of Psalm 20: "The Lord answer you in the day of trouble! The name of the God of Jacob protect you!" This verse gives us a hint at another possible translation for Jacob's name. His name could also mean "May God protect!" So, instead of trying to grab his brother in order to get ahead, Jacob could have stretched up and tried to grab God and God's protection. Everybody stretch up and try to get a hand on God: Reach for the heavens! Keep reaching up toward God, and let's have a prayer to thank God that we don't need to worry about getting ahead on our own; God will take care of us. (*Prayer.*)

BETHEL (*Jacob's Dream*)

Scripture: Genesis 28:10-22
Focus: The presence of God, whether we are "on the run" or safely in the house of the Lord, is always with us.
Experience: To help children "follow" Jacob by role-playing his flight from Beer-sheba to Bethel, to recall his dream as the children themselves sleep on real stones, and to make and anoint an altar to the Lord.
Arrangements: You will need a small, flat stone (4" to 6" across, available from many garden supply stores) for each child. Strew these around the area where you usually meet. Also have on hand a napkin or towel and some oil if you plan to anoint your "pillar."

LEADER: Will the children please meet me at the back of the sanctuary? Good morning! Today we're going to remember the story of Jacob. Jacob had to run away from his brother Esau after Jacob played a nasty trick on him. (*Start "running away" toward the usual meeting area.*) Let's pretend we're Jacob. Run along with me, but keep checking over your shoulder to make sure Esau isn't following. Finally Jacob had to stop for the night (*stop "running" when you arrive at your usual meeting place with the children*), and he was tired. He didn't have much with him—certainly not a pillow—so he found a stone and used that as a pillow. (*Have the children find a stone and lie down with it as a pillow.*) Comfortable?

CHILDREN: No!

L: No, well, Jacob probably wasn't either, because he had an amazing dream. Who knows what he dreamed?

C: About a ladder. About angels. (*If children don't remember, briefly describe the dream.*)

L: That's right, and then he heard God's voice. Does anyone know what God said to Jacob? God told Jacob not to be afraid, that God would be with him, and that God would keep all the promises to Jacob that God had made to Jacob's grandfather, Abraham, and to Jacob's father, Isaac. Well, when Jacob woke up, do you know what he said?

C: Good morning?

L: Hmmm. Probably so, but he also said, "Surely the Lord is in this place." And then he made a stack of some of those stones and poured oil over it to dedicate it to God. Maybe we can do that. (*Collect stones and fashion them into a pyramid-shaped "pillar" on the floor or on top of the communion table, and anoint it with oil. If you plan to anoint the stones, be sure to build the pillar on a towel or napkin, and use oil sparingly!*) Let's all say together what Jacob said: "Surely the Lord is in this place."

C: Surely the Lord is in this place.

L: Good! Let's have a prayer and give thanks that God is in this place, and in all the places of our lives. (*Prayer.*)

WHAT? (God Calls Young Samuel)

Scripture: 1 Samuel 3:1-10
Focus: The call of God is a unique and individual thing. The focus of this sermon is to affirm that we may hear God calling our hearts when we least expect it.
Experience: To simulate Samuel's call by having someone in the congregation call the name of one of the children three times, and sending the child to investigate. When the child is unable to discover the caller, you will explain how God calls us.
Arrangements: Choose someone to do the "calling," agree on which child's name will be called, and provide directions about when the calls are to come and how the caller can remain hidden from the child. Be sure to check before the service (or with the child's parents the night before) to make sure she/he is in church for the sermon.

LEADER: Well, hello! How is everyone today? Great to see you, and it's good that you all are here, because we have something very important to talk about . . . (*Provide cue to caller.*)

CALLER: Christopher!

L: What was that?

CHILDREN: Someone called Christopher!

L: (*Turning to Christopher*) Christopher, who would be calling you?

CHRISTOPHER: I don't know!

L: Well, you'd better go see so that we can continue. (*Child goes out into congregation.* In our case, Christopher is rather outspoken and so he demands . . .)

CHRISTOPHER: Who called me? (*And of course, no one answers!*)

L: Well, Christopher, come on back and we'll keep going. Now let's see, I said, "Good morning," and then I said we had something important to talk about, and . . . (*Cue caller.*)

CALLER: Christopher!

CHRISTOPHER: Oh brother!

L: Go ahead: see if you can find out who called. (*Christopher leaves to search, asks one or two people if they called him, returns with head shaking.*) Oh well, let's keep going. The important thing I want to talk to you about this morning is in the Bible, and . . . (*Cue caller.*)

CALLER: CHRISTOPHER!!!

CHILDREN: (*Giggles.*)

CHRISTOPHER: I know, I know, go and see who it is. (*Goes and returns with no luck.*)

L: Well, you know, this has worked out pretty well anyway, because I wanted to tell you about Samuel this morning. He was a young boy who served in the temple long ago. One night he kept hearing has name called, but he couldn't tell who it was. He thought it was the priest, but who do you think it turned out to be?

C: God? Jesus?

L: That's right, it was God. Sometimes God can call us, maybe not with a voice that we hear, like Christopher's caller, but in a special voice that speaks to our hearts. Let's have a prayer and give thanks that God sometimes calls our hearts and tells us how much we are loved. (*Prayer.*)

DANCE BEFORE THE LORD WITH ALL YOUR MIGHT
(*David Dances Near the Ark of God*)

Scripture: 2 Samuel 6:1-19
Focus: David's leaping and dancing as the ark of God was brought into Jerusalem was no doubt an expression of pure joy. We, too, can use our bodies to express the same kind of joy before God.
Experience: To have children try different kinds of dancing as a means of laughing together, and then to experience a joyful, whirling, leaping dance as a kind of prayer before the Lord.
Arrangements: None are needed, unless you care to stretch as a warm-up exercise!

LEADER: (*After reading the scripture selection*) Good morning! Let's all meet out here in the aisle where we have a little more room. Great! I'm wondering about the story we just heard. It says that "David and all the house of Israel were dancing before the Lord with all their might, with songs and lyres and harps and tambourines and castanets and cymbals" (2 Samuel 6:5). What kind of dance do you suppose David and the children of Israel did?

CHILDREN: (*Silence.*)

L: Do you suppose it was a hula? Let's all hula. . . . That's good, do you suppose that was the dance they did?

C: No!

L: OK, how about a square dance? Let's all swing our partners. . . . (*Do a few steps.*) Do you think that's what they were doing, a square dance?

C: No!

L: Hmmm. I know, since they had castanets, maybe they were doing the Mexican Hat Dance! That's it. Everybody stamp your heels, and pretend to dance around a hat, Olé! You don't think it was the Mexican Hat Dance, do you?

C: No.

L: Well, the children of Israel probably weren't doing that either. In fact, the word that the Bible uses here for "dance" can also be translated as "skip, whirl, and leap." Let's try that; maybe it's kind of like what ice skaters do when they jump up in the air and turn around. (*Let the children have a few practice tries.*) Like jumping for joy, isn't it?

C: Yes!

L: Well, that's exactly what David and all his people were doing. They were jumping for joy, dancing with all their might because they were so happy and joyful about what God was doing in their lives. Let's have a prayer and tell God how joyful we are. And for our prayer, let's do our whirl dance once more. Everybody ready? Let's pray. (*Jump up and turn.*) Amen!

WHICH VOICE?
(Elijah Hears the Still, Small Voice)

Scripture: 1 Kings 19:11-18
Focus: Our world is noisy. It is easy to be confused by what is and what is not God's voice. The focus of this sermon is how God can speak to us in times of silence and quiet.
Experience: To experience Elijah's time in the cave, waiting for a voice he recognized as God's.
Arrangements: None are needed.

LEADER: Hello! Let's all meet out here where we have some more room. (*Have children move to a wide aisle or large, open space.*) We just heard the story about Elijah going to a cave to wait until he heard God. We need someone to be Elijah (*choose child*), and the rest of us need to make a circle that can be Elijah's cave. *(Have children form a circle.)* Now let's have Elijah go inside. Good. The first thing that Elijah heard while he listened for God's voice was a strong wind. Let's make the sound of a strong wind. Congregation, you can help us with this. Everybody make the sound of a strong wind.

CHILDREN AND CONGREGATION: Whooooosh.

L: That was good! And was that the voice of God?

C: No!

L: No. Then the next thing Elijah heard was the sound of an earthquake. Let's have an earthquake! (*Start stamping your feet and making rumbling noises.*)

C AND C: (*Stamp feet, rumbling sounds.*)

L: And was God in the earthquake?

C: No!

L: No. And then Elijah heard fire. Can we make a fire sound? (*Make crackling sounds.*)

C AND C: Crackle, crackle, crackle.

L: Well, that's better than I thought! And was God in the fire?

C: No.

L: No. And then Elijah heard a still, small voice. (*Raise your finger to your lips; long pause of silence.*) And when Elijah heard it, he came out of the cave and listened to God. (*Bring Elijah out of the circle.*) Let's have a prayer and give thanks that we can hear God's voice in silence. (*Prayer—start with another long pause of silence if desired.*)

LET YOUR "YES" BE "YES"
(Section from Jesus' "Sermon on the Mount")

Scripture: Matthew 5:33-37

Focus: Covenants and promises are things we live into. In other words, we seldom know what challenges we may face when we say, "I promise." The focus of this sermon is on being faithful to our promises—to God and to others—even when the situation changes.

Experience: To make a promise to walk to the end of the aisle and back, only to have the aisle fill up with people, making the promise more difficult to keep.

Arrangements: None are needed.

LEADER: Look at you all. It's so good to see everybody! I wonder if you all would be willing to promise to do something for me. Would you be willing, in just a moment, to walk down the aisle to the back doors of the church and then walk back? If you would be willing to make that promise, say "yes."

CHILDREN: Yes.

L: That's great. (*Turn toward the congregation*) Would the congregation please stand? And now would you all please move into the aisle? (*The adults fill the aisle.*)

C: Hey!

L: Are you still willing to keep your promise?

C: Yes.

L: OK, go ahead. (*You may need to remind children that it isn't a race or a shoving match, in deference to your congregation's toes! After children return, ask the congregation to return to their seats.*) You kept your promise, but it was a little harder than you thought when you first said "yes," wasn't it?

C: Yes!

L: That happens to us a lot in our life. We make a promise—sometimes to God, sometimes to other people—and we really mean to keep it. But then something changes or things get tough, and we have a really hard time trying to keep our promise. Let's have a prayer and thank God for giving us the strength to keep our promises, to let our "yes" mean "yes." (*Prayer.*)

THE LAST WILL BE FIRST
(Jesus' Parable about the Kingdom of God)

Scripture: Matthew 20:1-16

Focus: The strange logic of the Kingdom of God is always a test for us. In the text at hand, Jesus suggests that God's gifts are the result of love for us, not of our ability to earn them.

Experience: To be part of a group that performs a task and gets paid according to a prearranged agreement, but differently from another group that performs the same task.

Arrangements: You will need to have candy or whatever else you might want to use as "payment." Also, decide on the distance you will ask the various groups to travel as part of their "task": if it will take too long to make three trips around your sanctuary, lay out another course. Finally, alert ushers to help wayward travelers!

LEADER: Good morning! Oh, we've got work to do, work to do! I need you children (*indicate about one-third of the group*) to go around the sanctuary (*or some shorter distance*) three times. If you do that, I'll give you each three pieces of candy. Are you willing to do that?

CHILDREN: Yes.

L: Great, go ahead. (*After they've gone*) Now, I need you children (*indicate another third*) to go around the sanctuary (*or other*) two times, and if you do that I'll give you three pieces of candy. OK?

C: OK!

L: Go ahead. (*After they've gone, say to remaining children*) And will all of you be willing to go around the sanctuary (*or other*) one time? If you do, I'll give you each three pieces of candy.

C: (*They leave.*)

L: (*Hopefully all three groups will finish more or less at the same time. Wait until everyone is there before making payments.*) That was great! Group number one: three laps around the sanctuary, three pieces of candy. One, two, three. Group number two: two laps around the sanctuary, three pieces of candy. One, two, three.

C: Hey . . .

L: (*Ignoring complaints for now*) And group number three: one trip around the sanctuary, three pieces of candy. One, two, three.

C: That's not fair!

L: (*If no one complains ask, "Is that fair?" Response will probably be "No!"*) Well, didn't you agree to make the three trips for
three pieces of candy?

C: Yeah, but *they* didn't go around three times.

L: Well, that wasn't the deal with them. But you know, the way
you're feeling right now is a lot like the people probably felt in a
story Jesus told about some workers who were just like us. Some
did less work than others, but everyone got paid the same. It was
Jesus' way of telling us that God gives us all the same amount of
love, no matter what we do or who we are. That's good news, because usually we're not the ones who have worked the longest, but
who have worked the shortest and deserve the least. It's a hard thing
to understand, but that's the way God's love is. God loves everyone
equally; and God loves us a lot! Let's have a prayer to thank God for
loving us no matter how much or how little we deserve it. (*Prayer.*)

GO AND MAKE DISCIPLES (*Jesus' Great Commission*)

Scripture: Matthew 28:18-20
Focus: The last words of Jesus command us to make disciples. This
sermon focuses on one way in which we can do that.
Experience: To be hugged as we move through a "disciple-making
machine," and then to set up our own "machine."
Arrangements: None are needed, although you may want to identify
ahead of time six or eight adults who will be your "disciple-making
machine." These people will stand face to face in two parallel lines,
becoming a kind of tunnel or assembly line for the children to pass
through.

LEADER: Good to see you all. I've got a question for you: What is
a disciple?

CHILDREN: A follower of Jesus. Someone who loves Jesus.

L: Those are good answers. And the Bible tells us to make disciples. So my next question is: How do we make disciples?

C: (*Puzzled silence.*)

L: Well, it just so happens that we have a disciple-making machine here at church! Will you all please get in a line, and will my

disciple-making machine

disciple-making machinery please come forward? (*Give directions to adults if they were not instructed earlier.*) This is one of our church disciple-making machines. Here is the entrance and here is where you come out. (*Indicate an "entrance" at one end of the parallel lines of adults and an "exit" at the other end.*) And what happens when you come into the machine (*begin guiding children in*) is that you get hugged by everyone you pass. (*Adults should hug each child as she or he moves through. Meanwhile, continue to explain . . .*)

This is a machine made up of people who are already disciples. They know that disciples are made when they discover how much Jesus loves them. And we can show them how much Jesus loves them by obeying his commandment to love one another. That's how we make disciples. When we've come through to the other end of the machine, we can join in and become part of it. (*Have children extend the lines of adults and hug their peers who are still coming down the line.*)

(*Once everyone is through*) Let's hold hands and thank God that we can learn how to be a disciple from other disciples who love us, and that we can help make disciples by loving other people, too. (*Prayer.*)

IN THE WILDERNESS
(*The Temptation of Jesus*)

Scripture: Mark 1:9-13
Focus: We live in a world that challenges us. There are "wilderness" periods in our lives: times of emptiness, loneliness, fear, and anxiety often trouble us. The focus of this sermon is to explore how Jesus used his time of solitude in the wilderness to pray and meditate.
Experience: To recreate the wilderness and then have forty seconds of silence and prayer. For most of the children in this setting, the time will feel like forty days!
Arrangements: None are needed, but a sweep-hand watch will help you be sure to time a full forty seconds. (It really does feel like a long time!)

LEADER: Good to see you all! In the story we just heard, it says that after Jesus was baptized "the Spirit drove him into the wilderness." We're going to try to go with Jesus into the wilderness this morning to see what it might have been like for him. First of all, we need to create a wilderness. Let's see, you (*pointing to a nearby adult in the congregation*) and you (*another*): Can you come up here and be, hmmm, you look like trees to me. Not beautiful, lush trees, but the scary kind of trees you see in a wilderness. Now we need some bushes. How about if all of you (*indicating a family of four*) come up here and be bushes? (*Work to arrange this landscape in such a way that it will encircle the children when they "enter" it.*) What else? Oh, how about some rocks? We need some rock-like people. You, sir, and you, and maybe you. (*Choose people to be rocks and position them in the "wilderness circle." Then say to children*) Does that look like a good wilderness?

CHILDREN: Yes. No. The rocks keep moving.

L: Well, that's the wilderness we're going to enter, just as Jesus did. (*Guide children into wilderness.*) Do you remember what the story said Jesus did here?

C: Talked to Satan. Was hungry. Was tempted.

L: That's right, all those things. And because of all that, he prayed. And he didn't just pray a little. He stayed in the wilderness and prayed for forty days. We don't have that long, but let's get on our knees, and I'll time forty seconds. Can we be silent and pray for that long?

c: Yes.

L: Let's give it a try. (*Pause for forty seconds of silent prayer.*) Amen.

PEACE, BE STILL!
(Jesus Stills the Storm)

Scripture: Mark 4:35-41

Focus: There is a transcendence in stillness, especially when it is preceded by commotion. The focus of this sermon is on the power of Jesus to create stillness out of chaos.

Experience: To imagine ourselves in the boat with Jesus, to go through the storm, and to come into the stillness Jesus commands. The congregation will create a "rainstorm" using the sound effects described below.

Arrangements: None are necessary.

LEADER: Good morning! Will the children please meet me in the middle of the church? Are you ready to go sailing today?

CHILDREN: Yes!

L: Good! Let's all sit down and imagine that we're in a boat with Jesus as it goes across the Sea of Galilee. We'll need someone to be Jesus. OK, Bradley. It says in the Bible that Jesus went to the back of the boat and fell asleep. Good, just lie down there and take a nap; we'll get back to you. It also says in the Bible that while they were going across, a great storm arose. Congregation, can you rub your hands together to make a sound like gently falling rain?

CONGREGATION: (*Rub hands together.*)

L: That's good. And now the rain starts falling harder, so snap your fingers to sound like big raindrops plopping.

c: (*Snap fingers.*)

L: And I imagine the boat was starting to rock a bit, so those of us in the boat need to start feeling those waves. (*Begin rocking motion with children, then continue excitedly.*) And then the rain started falling really hard. So, congregation, pat your knees. And the wind was blowing, so make wind sounds. (*Pause briefly for congregation's sound effects.*) And the boat started rocking harder (*exaggerate rocking motion*), and the thunder boomed (*cue congregation*), and the rain fell, and the wind blew, and the boat rocked. And the disciples started to get worried. (*You may be yelling by now, to be heard above the storm going on in the sanctuary; but that's fine, it will add to the effect!*) And they went to wake up Jesus. Somebody wake up Jesus. And they said, "Teacher . . . " (*Cue children.*)

C: TEACHER!

L: Don't you care that we're going to die?

C: Don't you care that we're going to die?

L: And the rain was falling, and the wind was blowing, and the boat was rocking. And then Jesus said, "Peace, be still." (*Cue child who is playing Jesus.*)

JESUS: Peace, be still.

L: (*Cut congregation off with a big motion. Then pause for several seconds to experience the silence.*) Wow! Think of how relieved and impressed the disciples must have felt. Let's have a prayer and thank God that even the wind and the sea obey Jesus. (*Prayer.*)

I BELIEVE (Jesus Heals a Man's Son)

Scripture: Mark 9:14-29
Focus: *Saying* what we believe is an important part of reminding ourselves that we *do* believe. The focus of this sermon is to value and acknowledge those things the children believe in.
Experience: To write an affirmation of faith (or confession of faith) using things the children say they believe about God, and adding the phrase from the father in the Scripture, "I believe, help my unbelief!"
Arrangements: A flip chart, newsprint, or overhead and marking pen. You may also want to arrange to use the creed produced by the children at the appropriate time in worship.

LEADER: It's so good to see you all this morning! You know, every week we have a time in worship when we say what we believe about God. Sometimes we use the Apostles' Creed, sometimes we use the Nicene Creed or some other creed or confession. A creed is a statement of our beliefs. And all of those creeds came from people who wrote down what they believed. I thought that this morning we might make our own list of things we believe about God (and then use it in worship later today). I'll act as your secretary. At the top of this piece of paper I'll write the words, "I Believe" (*pause to do so*) and you can tell me what you believe about God.

CHILDREN: Jesus is alive. Jesus died for me. God loves me. Jesus is my friend. (*Add each item as children express their beliefs. Be sure to print neatly and in large letters.*)

L: That's a wonderful list of things to believe. I think the only thing we need to add to it are the father's words from the Bible story we read a few minutes ago: "I believe; help my unbelief." That will cover anything else we might have missed, and it will ask God to help us believe even more. (*Have congregation stand and read the creed you have written, or arrange for the congregation to use it later in worship.*)

Let's have a prayer and thank God for giving us such good things to believe in. (*Prayer.*)

WHERE ARE YOU GOING?
(*The Road to Emmaus*)

Scripture: Luke 24:13-27
Focus: The Christian faith is often represented as a journey. The focus of this sermon is to utilize this helpful metaphor in a way that children can understand, noting especially that Jesus is "on the road" with us.
Experience: To "walk through" a typical week in the children's lives.
Arrangements: You will need pictures of children's home, school, friends, extended family, and church. You might want to ask children ahead of time (contact them during the week or during Sunday School hour) to draw these five pictures, or you could ask someone

home

school

friends

extended
family

church

else to draw them on large sheets of paper (See examples on p. 34). The picture of the church should have a border with small crosses drawn around the church (enough crosses to supply each child with one). The crosses will be cut off at the end of the sermon and distributed to the children. You will also need scissors to clip the crosses off the picture.

LEADER: Good morning! Let's meet out in the middle of the aisle this morning. (*Distribute the five pictures to congregation members along aisle while talking to children.*) In the Bible story we just read, Jesus met two men while they were on a journey. This morning we're going to take a little journey, a trip through the week, to see when and where we meet Jesus. Where are you usually when you wake up on Monday morning?

CHILDREN: At home in bed.

L: OK, let's go to the picture over here of the house. (*Lead children to the person who's holding up the house picture.*) This is home. Now, where do most of you go from home?

C: School.

L: Right, so we'll journey over to the picture of school. (*Lead children to picture.*) After school where do you go?

C: Day care. Grandma's (or other relative's). Back home. My friend's house.

L: Hmmm. All right, some of us go to Grandma's: that's the house over there (*send some children to picture representing home of extended family*), some go to our friend's house (*send some to picture representing friend's house*). And all of us, even if we make an extra stop along the way, eventually end up back at our own home. (*Take remaining children back to "home" picture.*) Everyone else come on back here, too. All right! Tuesday morning when you wake up, what happens?

C: Go to school!

L: You go to school again. After school, some go to friends' homes, some to Grandma's, and eventually all of us get back home again. Next day is . . .

C: Wednesday!

L: Right (*speeding up now in an exaggerated way*): up from bed, over to school, Grandma's, friend's, back home. Thursday: up, school, everybody go to a friend's house today, back home. Friday (*even faster*): school, Grandma's today, home. Saturday: up—hurray—no school! Go to friend's, go back home. Sunday: up, where to?

c: Church!

L: Where's the church picture? Over there. Everyone go to church. (*Lead all children to church picture.*) Stay at church a while, then, let's go visit Grandma again, and then back home again. Whew! That's a busy week! But you know what? Don't you feel maybe something is wrong with our journey? What's the most important place we went?

c: School? Church?

L: I think it's the church. But where did we spend the least amount of time?

c: Church.

L: What can we do? (*Begin cutting crosses from border of church picture and distribute these to children.*) Did you know that no matter where we go on our journey, Jesus is always with us on the way? Whether we are at home or at school or at a friend's house or Grandma's house or piano lessons or anywhere, Jesus is there too. Let's have a prayer to thank Jesus for always being with us on our journey. (*Prayer.*)

GO AND BEAR FRUIT
(*Jesus' Command to Love One Another*)

Scripture: John 15:12-17
Focus: Just as the life cycle of a plant is not complete until it has dropped its fruit containing the seed for a new generation, so our life in Christ is not fulfilled until we bear the fruit of love—a fruit that attracts others to know Christ as well. The focus of this sermon is fruit-bearing.
Experience: To go through the life cycle of a plant. You will ask children to imitate you as you pantomime the growth of a plant.
Arrangements: None are needed.

LEADER: Good morning! You all look like you could just sprout up and burst into bloom. And that's a good thing, because I want to ask you: How do plants grow? What do they start with?

CHILDREN: A seed.

L: A seed, that's right. Let's all get into a little ball shape, as if we were a seed in the ground. Now, is this all there is to a plant?

C: No!

L: No; next, the seed sends up a little sprout. (*Ask children to imitate you as you lift one arm upward.*) Now is the plant finished growing?

C: No. It needs roots.

L: Oh, I forgot about roots! OK, let's grow some roots. (*Put other arm down, fingers spread.*) Now is the plant finished?

C: No. Yes.

L: Not quite yet! The sprout grows taller and becomes a plant. (*Stand up, arms outstretched like branches.*) Now is the plant finished?

C: Yes.

L: Nope! There's more for that plant to do! Next, the plant needs to bear fruit. (*Shape hands into a ball.*) Do you think it's finished now?

C: Yes? No?

L: No, there's one last thing. That plant has to drop its fruit on the ground, because that fruit has seeds in it for another plant. (*Open hands, as if dropping seed.*) And do you know what? Jesus' followers are a little bit like a plant. Just like a plant, we grow into better and better followers of Jesus. He helps us do that. And, just like a plant, we need to bear seeds that can help other people become Jesus' followers as well. Do you know what those seeds are?

C: No.

L: They are the love we show to others. When we are kind and loving to others, they can begin to see how much Jesus loves them. And then they can love Jesus and become his followers, too. Let's have a prayer to thank God for helping us bear fruit by loving other people and planting seeds of Jesus' love in them. (*Prayer.*)

PSALMS

GROANING

Scripture: Psalm 22:1 (see also Exodus 2:23-25; Judges 2:18; Romans 8:22-23)
Focus: Prayer is so much more than asking God for things. At the same time, sometimes we don't even know what we need to ask for. The Bible suggests that we have an Intercessor who prays for us with sighs or groans too deep for words.
Experience: To experiment with using several sounds as a prayer, and to examine groaning as a fine way to pray at times.
Arrangements: None are needed.

LEADER: Howdy! How's everyone doing?

CHILDREN: Fine!

L: Well, good. Listen, I've been a little confused lately, and I need your help. Is this a good way to pray? (*Whistle or hum a few notes. Have children imitate you.*)

C: No!

L: How about this—is *this* a good way to pray? (*Make honking sound; have children imitate.*)

C: NO!

L: Well, what about this? (*Make any other silly sound you can think of; have children imitate.*)

C: NOOOO!

L: All right, last one: What about this? (*Groan; have children imitate.*)

C: No.

L: Well, actually, that can be a good way to pray. The Bible tells us that a groan is a prayer God recognizes! Listen to what it says in the book of Psalms: "My God, my God, why have you forsaken me? Why are you so far from helping me, from the words of my groaning?" (Psalm 22:1). So God does hear us when we groan! Let's try groaning together again.

C: (*Groan.*)

L: That was really good. What kind of prayer is that? Is it a prayer that says, "Thanks, God, everything is great with me"?

C: No!

L: Might it be a prayer that says, "Oh, God, I'm sad and I need help"?

C: Yes!

L: Well, let's have a prayer to give thanks that God understands even our sad and groaning prayers. When I'm finished giving thanks, we'll all say a groan prayer together. Think of something that makes you sad, that you might want to groan about to God. Then, when you make your groaning prayer, you can silently also tell God what is making you sad and ask for God's help. (*Prayer of thanks, then groaning prayer.*)

IT'S OK TO PRAY WITH A MOTION

Scripture: Psalm 25
Focus: Prayer can be difficult to understand even for the most senior saints, especially the kind of prayer that is more than just asking God for things. The focus of this sermon is on the variety of prayers and ways of praying.
Experience: To use a series of motions to indicate different ways of praying, as suggested by Psalm 25.
Arrangements: None are needed.

LEADER: Good morning! Everyone looks prayerful today. What kinds of prayers do you sometimes say?

CHILDREN: Bless the food. Bless my mommy and daddy. Ask God for things.

L: All of those are good prayers. They make me think that there are different kinds of prayers for different kinds of things. Sometimes we want to thank God for things, sometimes we want to tell God we're sorry for something we did, sometimes we want to ask God to help us, and sometimes we just need to sit still and wait for God to say something to us. Would you like to learn a way to remember all of that?

C: (*Nod agreement.*)

L: The very first thing we should do when we pray is to get quiet and wait, so let's just sit and fold our hands on our lap

(Psalm 25:1-3—waiting). That's good. Next, we might ask God for what we need, so we could raise our folded hands up in the air, almost as if we were begging (Psalm 25:4-5—intercession). That's great. After we do that, we might remember that we have things we need to confess to God, so why don't we make two fists and put them on our heads as if we were really sorry (Psalm 25:6-7—confession). But the good news is that if we confess our sins, God forgives us. And not just that, but God gives us blessings on top of blessings. So let's thank God by opening up our hands and raising them high in the air (Psalm 25:8-10—praise). Doesn't that feel happy and thankful? And then, we can bring our hands back down into our laps as they were at first, and just be still and wait for God (Psalm 25:21—waiting). Good, let's do all of them again in order: waiting, asking, confessing, praising, waiting. (*Move through motions while saying these key words.*) Do you think those movements will help you when you pray?

C: Yes.

L: Well then, let's pray! (*Lead everyone, perhaps even the whole congregation, in a silent or spoken prayer with motions for waiting, asking, confessing, praising, and waiting for God to answer. You might want to read aloud sections of Psalm 25 that mention these actions: verses 1, 4, 5, 16-18, 20.*)

HOLY HANDS (*The Lord's Supper or Baptism*)

Scripture: Psalm 28:2; 63:4; 134:2; 141:2, 143:6
Focus: Worship is an activity that can involve the whole person, including our bodies. This is true as we sing, as we pass communion plates and offering plates to one another, as we stand and sit, as we shake hands and hug, just to name a few examples. The focus of this sermon is on the use of our hands in worship, as we learn an invitation to prayer.
Experience: To learn simple hand motions to accompany the words to the invitation to prayer used in some traditions before communion and/or baptism. This can be especially effective if the entire congregation participates with the hand motions, when the invitation is used later in worship before communion or baptism.
Arrangements: None are needed.

LEADER: Good to see everyone! Today I'd like for us to learn some hand motions that go along with words we sometimes say before special prayers. How many of you have heard me (or the minister) say, "The Lord be with you"?

CHILDREN: Me! I have!

L: Do you know what the congregation says next?

C: And you. And also with you. And be with you, too.

L: That's right; they say, "And also with you." Well, today I'm going to hold my hands open, turn my palms up, and stretch my arms toward you when I say, "The Lord be with you." (*Demonstrate as you speak.*) And then I'd like you to make the same motion back toward me while you say, "And also with you."

C: (*Make motion.*) And also with you.

L: That's great! Next I'm going to keep my hands open, my palms up, and my hands out, but now I'm going to raise them upward and say, "Lift up your hearts." (*Demonstrate as you speak.*) And then I'd like you to lift your hands as you say, "We lift them up to the Lord."

C: (*Make motion.*) We lift them up to the Lord.

L: That's really good. And finally, I'll bring my hands down and fold them for prayer while I say, "Let us give thanks to the Lord our God." (*Demonstrate.*) And then you can do the same while you say, "It is right to give thanks and praise."

C: (*Make motion.*) It is right to give thanks and praise.

L: Good, now let's try the whole thing. (*Repeat, using motions. Then close with prayer.*)

HIDE AND SEEK (*The Lord's Supper*)

Scripture: Psalm 32

Focus: It must be human nature to want to hide our sins. At best, it keeps us from probable embarrassment; at worst, it keeps us from fully recognizing God's invitation to receive grace and forgiveness. The focus of this sermon is on the futility of hiding from an all-knowing God whose will it is to invite us to the Table to receive forgiveness.

Experience: To try to hide from God and see how foolish this is.

Arrangements: None are needed, but it wouldn't be a bad idea to let the ushers know what you're up to so they can keep children from leaving the building! For the last part of the sermon, children will gather around the altar or table for the Lord's Supper.

LEADER: How are we all doing today? It's great to see everybody. You all look so sweet and innocent, but I have a question for you: Have you ever done something wrong—broken a friend's toy, for instance—and then tried to hide it so they wouldn't know?

CHILDREN: Yes. No. I lost my daddy's hammer outside last week.

L: Well, a lot of other people have tried to hide their wrong actions, too. It says right in the beginning of the Bible that after Adam and Eve sinned they tried to hide themselves so God wouldn't know. You know, I bet we all did something wrong this week. Maybe we should try to hide from God. Everybody go on and hide, but stay in the church.

C: (*With giggles, go and hide.*)

L: (*After allowing enough time for them to hide*) Wait a minute! Can we hide from God? NO! God can see us wherever we are. When you play hide-and-seek, what do you say when it's safe to come out?

C: Ollie, ollie oxen free (*or whatever*).

L: But do you know what God says? "Come to the Table." Everyone come out and come back up here and gather around the altar (table). Because of what Jesus did for us, we have this special meal as a reminder that we don't need to try to hide from God. God still loves us and promises to forgive us, no matter what we do. Let's have a prayer and give thanks that God loves us and invites us to come and be safe here. (*Prayer.*)

LONGING

Scripture: Psalm 42
Focus: The psalmist suggests that our souls thirst for God the way a deer thirsts for flowing streams. The focus of this sermon is to experience thirst and relief from thirst. While the children may not now understand the parallel, plant the idea that a similar truth exists for our souls.
Experience: With the children, pretend you are deer, and wander around the sanctuary, getting thirstier and thirstier until you finally find water to drink.
Arrangements: Have on hand a tray with cups of water for the children.

LEADER: Good to see you today. Let's stand up, and let's pretend we are deer. We are deer walking around the . . . where do deer live?

CHILDREN: In the woods. In the forest.

L: (*Start walking around sanctuary.*) Let's pretend we are deer walking around the woods. We are deer out for a walk. But you know what? It's a hot day in this forest, and the farther we walk, the thirstier we get. Let's pretend we are getting thirsty. What do deer do when they get thirsty?

C: Drink? My dog sticks out his tongue.

L: I bet deer stick out their tongues, too. That's called panting (*stick out your tongue and pant*), and I bet they look for something to drink. Meanwhile, we're still walking around the woods; and the longer we walk, the thirstier we get. Walking. Thirstier. Walking. Thirstier. Panting. Thirstier. (*By now you have led the children close to where the water is.*) What is it that a deer would want to drink?

C: Water?

L: Really good water, wouldn't that taste great right now? And we just happen to have some right here. (*Pass out water.*) AHHH! You know, in the Bible it says that sometimes our soul gets thirsty. What's a soul?

C: Your insides. Where God lives. What goes to heaven when you die.

L: That's right, our soul is a special part of us that is close to God. But sometimes, especially if we've kept God out of our soul, it gets thirsty. What do you think your soul would want to drink?

C: (*Puzzled silence; then at last*) Water?

L: A very special kind of water called "living water." And we get that special, living water when we pray to Jesus and ask him to be with us. Let's give thanks that God sends the living water of Jesus to make our souls no longer thirsty. (*Prayer.*)

1 JOHN

I FORGIVE *YOU*!

Scripture: 1 John 1:1-10
Focus: One of the mysteries of Christian community is that, for it to survive, we must forgive one another. But this mystery is preceded by an even deeper mystery, one that we too often overlook: We can only forgive one another as we individually understand and receive God's forgiveness. Each of us first has to recognize our need for forgiveness before we can offer authentic forgiveness to someone else.
Experience: To play a kind of tricky game designed to help children understand the importance of forgiving one another. In the game, each child will need to listen carefully in order to recognize that he or she is the one God has forgiven first.
Arrangements: Assign two adults or liturgists to speak the words of God's forgiveness, as given in the script below.

LEADER: Hello! Let's all meet in the aisle. Have you ever known people who couldn't get along together?

CHILDREN: Yes. My sister can't get along with me. Two boys at school had a fight last week. There was a fight at my school last week. I saw a fight on TV.

L: Well, obviously we've struck a chord here! Have you ever known people in the church who couldn't get along together? Not that they actually fought, but just that they didn't get along?

C: Yes. No.

L: Well, believe it or not, sometimes even people in the church don't get along. And today we're going to learn a way to help them when they don't get along. I want us to divide into two groups. Everyone over here make a line on this side of the aisle, and all of the rest of you make a line facing them on the other side of the aisle. (*If the aisle is in the center, each row will have its back to half the congregation. Ask an adult helper to stand at the head of each row.*) The key to getting along with one another in the church is to say to one another what we hear from God. That's what all of us need to do. First, each of you on this side (*indicate one side*) will tell the person next to you a wonderful promise that God has made to you. Listen as the adult in your row says God's promise aloud, then repeat it to the person next to you. (*Cue the adult helper.*)

ADULT HELPER: I forgive you.

C1: I forgive you.

L: Now the other side repeat what you hear God saying.

AH: I forgive you.

C2: I forgive you.

L: Who just got forgiven?

C: (*Each point to the other.*)

L: And who got forgiven first?

C: (*The first side will be indicated.*)

L: I'm not sure we've got it yet. Listen again to what God promises.

AH: I forgive YOU. (*Have helper emphasize* YOU.)

L: What did God say? Who was just forgiven by God?

C: Me?

L: That's right! Each one of us. We're the ones who are forgiven by God. And then, after we've heard God say it to us, we can say what we heard to someone else. That's the way it works! We can forgive someone else when we know we have been forgiven first. Let's have a prayer to thank God for forgiving us so that we can really forgive others and have a loving church family. (*Prayer.*)

WALK THE WALK

Scripture: 1 John 2:1-6
Focus: Learning how to walk the walk of a Christian means learning that walk from Jesus and from other people who know it.
Experience: To have fun trying to imitate some funny walks, and then to talk about how to know which people are good to imitate in life.
Arrangements: Invite three adults who would be willing to demonstrate a funny walk for the children to imitate. *Be sure each carries a Bible during their demonstration.*

LEADER: How is everyone doing today? I have a question for you: Who taught you how to walk?

CHILDREN: My mommy. Daddy. Sister. My dog. No one.

L: Well, you may not know it, but all of us learned to walk by watching other people, lots of other people. Even though every-one walks a little differently, each one taught us a little something more about how to walk. We learned by trying to imitate all these different walks. I've invited a few of our members to show us how they walk, and I thought we might try to imitate their way of walking. Here's Jim.

JIM: (*A big man who walks like a bear doing the rumba.*)

L: Great! That was Jim's walk. Let's see if we can walk like that!

C: (*Lots of giggles and laughs as they try.*)

L: Next is Lois.

LOIS: (*A walk that looks like Frankenstein's monster meets Godzilla.*)

L: Everybody ready? Let's try Lois's walk.

C: (*More fun.*)

L: And finally, Tom.

TOM: (*This one looks like a rabbit.*)

C: (*Imitate.*)

L: Well, some of us came pretty close to walking like they walked, but even the best of us didn't walk exactly like they did. Why not?

C: They were too hard.

L: They were hard, but there was something else. Did you notice that each one of them held a Bible while they walked? Even though this was a kind of silly exercise, it can teach us something important. As we watch other people to learn how to walk and how to live, we should always look at them carefully and make sure they're holding on to God's Word in their life! That way we know that they are people we should imitate. Let's thank God for people whose lives we can imitate and learn from as we try to learn how to walk in God's paths. (*Prayer.*)

WHOSE CHILDREN ARE WE?

Scripture: 1 John 3:1
Focus: Being someone's child has an effect on the way we see ourselves and the way we act. A strong emphasis of Christian theology is that we are all children of God. The focus of this sermon is how our behavior is affected by being children of God.
Experience: To pantomime different ways of acting based on pretend parents, and to talk about how we will act as God's children.
Arrangements: None are needed.

LEADER: Good morning! Let me ask you a question. Do you think that who your mother or father is means anything about how you are expected to act?

CHILDREN: (*Silence.*)

L: Well, for example, let's pretend that one of our parents was a general in the army. Do you think that you would have to act a certain way?

C: You'd have to follow orders?

L: That's right! And you might be expected to do other things too, like stand at attention. Well, let's get up and stand at attention!

C: (*Get up and stand at attention.*)

L: Good! OK, now let's pretend one of our parents is a movie star. How might we be expected to act?

C: Famous!

L: Right, let's see: How do famous people act? Maybe we could pretend we're signing autographs (*pretend to sign hand as if autographing*) and posing for pictures (*strike a pose with hand behind head, big smile*).

C: (*Children follow example.*)

L: Great! Now, what if one of our parents was the king or queen of England? How would we probably be expected to act?

C: (*May be no response.*)

L: I guess we'd be expected to act like British royalty. (*Assume a British accent.*) Yes, quite right. You know, it's about tea time (*pretend to hold tea cup*). Quite! Let's keep those pinkies out!

C: (*Children follow example.*)

L: Well, did you know that we don't have to pretend to be any of those kind of children? It says in the Bible that we are all children of God. And if God is our Father, I guess we are expected to act the way God acts. How does God act?

C: Good. Holy. Loves us.

L: All of those are good answers, and one way we can act like God—the way God wants us to act—is to love one another. Let's all give each other hugs so we can act like God's children.

C: (*Hug one another.*)

L: That's wonderful. Let's thank God that we're all God's children. (*Prayer.*)

LOVE IN TRUTH AND ACTION

Scripture: 1 John 3:18
Focus: In more than one Scripture text, the biblical writers suggest that "faith by itself, if it has no works, is dead" (James 2:17). From John's words about this subject, we can discover how the love we profess can be translated into action.
Experience: To meet several groups of people in the sanctuary, each of whom has a special need that the children will be able to meet.
Arrangements: You will need to ask a Sunday school class or a group of adults to divide into four clusters of two or more people and take up positions at places around the sanctuary as you begin the sermon. If the sanctuary is too large for these groups to go to the corners, perhaps they can be spaced along an aisle or across the front of the church. Each group should know roughly what you expect of them (see dialogue following). Feel free to invent needs different from those given below, reflecting your local situation and mission priorities. Give some thought, however, to how you will help the children meet the needs. For example, if one of the needs is hunger, make sure you or the children have a candy bar or can of food handy. Similarly, a cup of water could meet the need of a thirsty group.

LEADER: Good morning! I'd like to read a verse from the first Letter of John. Listen to what it says: "Little children, let us love, not in word or speech, but in truth and action" (1 John 3:18). What is John trying to say to us?

CHILDREN: That we should love.

L: That we should love. That's right, but he's saying that we should love in a special way. How are we supposed to love? (*It may be necessary to repeat the verse.*)

C: In words and speech?

L: Not just in words or speech. Did anyone hear anything else?

C: In action.

L: In action! That's right, by *doing* something. . . . Say, do you notice all these groups of people standing around the church? What do you suppose they're doing? Maybe we should go and talk to them. Maybe we can even love them in some way. (*Move to first group.*) Hello there, what seems to be the problem?

GROUP ONE SPEAKER: We're hungry. (*Holding stomach, others in group groan, etc.*)

L: You're hungry? (*To children*) If we tell them we love them, do you think that will fill them up?

C: No!

L: No! We can't just offer them words; we need to give them something else. Does anyone have a piece of candy in their pocket?

C: I have one.

L: Would you be willing to share it with these hungry people?

C: Yes. (*Gives candy away.*)

S: Thanks so very much!

L: That really was nice, but look, there's another group over there (*moving toward second group*), and they look pretty upset. What's the matter?

GROUP TWO SPEAKER: We're so sad (*crying*).

L: Oh my goodness! Well, let's just tell them to cheer up. Will that be all right?

C: No! Yes!

L: Well, it might be all right, but it might not be enough. How about if we give them all a hug? (*Begin hugging, encourage children to follow suit.*) That's great. Now look over there: more people (*moving to third group*) who might need our help. What's the matter with you all?

GROUP THREE SPEAKER: We're thirsty (*said with dry, whispery throat; others nod in agreement*).

L: Well, maybe one of us could go get a cup of water. (*Arrange with an usher to have a cup ready if this is not easily done by children.*) Will you go, Laura? And while she goes for water, I see one more group (*moving toward it*), and they seem pretty happy. What's going on here?

GROUP FOUR SPEAKER: We're celebrating, and we need someone to celebrate with us.

C: I will! I will!

L: Let's all celebrate with them. (*A few shouts of elation or quick jumps for joy, followed by . . .*) And now let's have a prayer of thanks to celebrate that God invites us to help one another not just with our words but by the things we do for them. (*Prayer.*)

PERSON TO PERSON (*Christmas*)

Scripture: 1 John 4:7-12
Focus: Just as God's love for us was made flesh in the person of Jesus Christ, so we can make God's love real for others by our actions of love toward them. It is as we truly love one another that "God lives in us, and his love is perfected in us" (1 John 4:12).
Experience: To try to love God by first hugging God, then by hugging (loving) others.
Arrangements: None are needed.

LEADER: Well, Merry Christmas! Why is this a special day? How does Christmas remind us that God loves us?

CHILDREN: He sent baby Jesus.

L: That's right, God showed us we are loved by sending Jesus Christ as a baby, as a person. It's as if God gave us a big hug by sending Jesus. Well, how do we show that we love God?

C: By being good, doing what God asks, giving presents. (*An inevitable response at this time of year!*)

L: That's all true. But I wonder . . . Have you ever hugged God?

C: (*Puzzled*) No.

L: Well, why don't we try? Everybody stand up and let's try to give God a big hug! (*Begin flapping your arms toward the skies and grabbing air, as if trying to hug someone much, much taller than you.*) Is this working? No! What are the problems with trying to hug God?

C: God is too big! God doesn't have a body. You can't see God.

L: Hmmm. Let's listen to a clue John gives us in the Bible: "since God loved us so much, we also ought to love one another . . . if we love one another, God lives in us, and his love is perfected in us" (1 John 4:11-12). John seems to be saying here in the Bible that by loving other people we are also showing our love for God. And when we do nice things for others, we help them see that God loves them—through us! So if we want to give God a hug, how could we do it?

C: By hugging other people?

L: That's right! Let's give it a try. (*Give hugs to people in the congregation and invite children to do so. Then reassemble the children.*) Let's have a prayer and give thanks that we can show how much we love God by loving the people around us. (*Prayer.*)

CHURCH YEAR

A LOT OF GRACE (*Advent*)

Scripture: Luke 1:5-13

Focus: Grace has a way of breaking in on us when we least expect it, surprising us with God's goodness. The focus of this sermon is on the unexpected grace that sometimes breaks into the routine of life.

Experience: The children will be involved in the casting and reading of "lots," similar to those used in Bible times. Each of the two lots will offer a cue for a song to be played by the organist. A surprise ending to the experience will lead to an understanding of the way God surprises us with a show of love.

Arrangements: You will need several materials to simulate the biblical use of the Urim and Thummim lots: two flat, similarly sized stones—one with the letter *U* marked on it, the other with the letter *T*; a jar or can with which to shake and toss the stones. You will want to ask the organist to be ready to play two simple melodies (for example, "Jesus Loves Me" and "Jingle Bells"), one when the Urim is cast, the other when Thummim is cast. The organist should also be ready to play the first few measures of a "big and flowery" piece—perhaps the "Hallelujah Chorus"—when you give the signal.

LEADER: Good morning! Let's talk about lots. Does anybody know what lots are?

CHILDREN: No.

L: Lots were something used in Bible times, especially in the Old Testament, to help people know what to do. Lots were probably two stones that looked a little like dice. When people had a question about what to do, the priest put the lots into a jar and prayed that God would use them to give an answer. Then the priest shook the jar until a lot fell out. If one lot came out, the people would do one thing; if the other came out, they'd do something else. We don't use lots in this way anymore, but this morning we'll try out some lots I made in order to know what song to sing. (*Shake out a stone from the jar.*) What letter is on this lot?

C: U.

L: (*To organist*) OK, that's the first song. (*Organist plays simple melody line for a few bars.*) Let's do it again. (*Replace stone in jar and shake until another pops out. If both come out, you can* *simply try again, or else go with the one that is face up with letter showing.)* Which one is that?

c: T.

(Organist plays second selection. Repeat the process five or six times, involving children in reading the lots. You might begin to show boredom and/or exasperation in your voice. On a prearranged cue for the organist—for example on the sixth throw— organist ignores the lot and breaks forth with a full-organ rendition of the "big and flowery" music selection.)

L: *(Showing surprise)* What was that? That wasn't one of the choices, was it?

c: NO!

L: What a wonderful surprise! We thought we were going to hear one song, but we heard something altogether different. And what we heard was even better than what we expected. Something like that happened to the priest Zechariah in today's Bible reading. He had been chosen by lot to work in the big temple at Jerusalem. And what that meant was that he'd go there just like all the other priests to pray and burn incense. But what a wonderful surprise Zechariah got. Something very special and unexpected happened. God sent an angel with wonderful news for Zechariah. God likes to surprise us, too. And the surprises are always so wonderful, like the way God sent Jesus to be born on the first Christmas. What a great surprise gift! Let's have a prayer to thank God for that. *(Prayer.)*

WAITING TOGETHER (Advent)

Scripture: Luke 1:39-56
Focus: "Waiting" is a theme that takes on great urgency during the Christian season of Advent. The focus of this sermon is on the fact that we don't wait alone, but rather with one another.
Experience: To talk to a person who is waiting, to find someone to wait with that person, to see how waiting is made easier and better when it is shared, and to understand that we don't have to be alone as we wait for Christmas.

Arrangements: This sermon works best when the "waiters" are two pregnant women; but with a little rewriting, you could make do with soon-to-graduate college or high school seniors, or with an engaged couple. Beforehand, briefly explain their roles to the "waiters" and rehearse some responses they might give.

LEADER: Will the children please come forward? (*As children come, one "waiter" moves to a central place on the chancel and sits.*) How are you all today? Is everybody excited about Christmas?

CHILDREN: Yes!

L: Christmas is so wonderful that it's kind of hard to wait for it to get here, isn't it?

C: Yes!

L: (*Pause and look around at "waiter" on chancel.*) Hmmm. I wonder what Ava is doing sitting over there. Should we ask her?

C: Yes.

L: (*To "waiter"*) What are you doing?

AVA: Waiting.

L: What are you waiting for?

AVA. Something very special.

L: Are you waiting all by yourself?

AVA: Yes.

L: That doesn't seem right. Let's see if we can't find someone else to wait with you. (*Send children to search for another woman who looks like first woman. Second woman should stand as children move near, or perhaps offer herself by saying, "I look like her . . . "*)

L: Well, Diane, you certainly do look like Ava! And you look like you might be waiting, too. Come up and sit a while by Ava. (*Ava and Diane begin to dialogue about challenges of being pregnant, about backaches and cravings, about excitement, about getting the nursery ready, and about whether they're expecting a boy or a girl. After a minute or two, Leader interrupts.*)

L: Well, I'm glad we helped Ava and Diane find someone to wait with. It sounded like they had a lot more fun waiting together. Do you remember what we said earlier that we were all waiting for?

c: Christmas!

l: Maybe it would be easier for us to wait together, too. Then we could talk about why it's hard to wait for Christmas, and what we are excited about, and what we expect might happen. (*Offer a chance for children to respond to any or all of these implied questions.*) Let's have a prayer to thank God that we have something so exciting to wait for, and that we don't have to wait for it alone. (*Prayer.*)

DO YOU HAVE BEAUTIFUL FEET? (*Advent*)

Scripture: Isaiah 52:7
Focus: The "good tidings" we bring at Advent and Christmas are words about Jesus Christ, who brings peace, offers salvation, and proclaims God's reign. This sermon takes a light-hearted look at the work of evangelism that we are all called to do.
Experience: To consider what makes our bare feet beautiful from a biblical perspective.
Arrangements: None are needed, but you might want to make sure you don't have on "holy" socks!

LEADER: Good morning! I have an important question for you today: Do you have beautiful feet?

CHILDREN: (*Giggle.*) Yes. No. What?

l: I guess there's really only one way to find out if we have beautiful feet or not, and that's to take off our shoes and socks, and take a careful look at our feet!

c: (*More giggles, begin taking off shoes and socks.*)

l: That's right (*taking off own shoes and socks*), take off those shoes while your parents hope you have on matching socks without holes. (*Allow time for children to remove shoes and socks. Then, while sitting down, extend your own feet and examine them while wiggling your toes. Encourage children to do the same.*) Good! Well, what do you think, do you have beautiful feet?

c: No! They're smelly! Gross!

l: I'm sure there are no smelly or gross feet here. In fact, all of these feet are beautiful—or at least they can be. According to the

Bible, what makes feet beautiful is the way they help us get around to tell people about Jesus and how much he loves them. Listen again to what Isaiah says in the Bible: "How beautiful upon the mountains are the feet of the messenger who announces peace, who brings good news, who announces salvation, who says to Zion, 'Your God reigns' " (Isa. 52:7). Let's all say another message of good news: "Jesus loves you."

C: Jesus loves you.

L: Do you think you can use your feet to walk up to others and tell them about Jesus' love?

C: Yes.

L: Do your feet look any more beautiful?

C: No.

L: Well, try saying the good news again, and say it like you mean it!

C: JESUS LOVES YOU.

L: Now, let's ask the congregation: Are these beautiful feet?

CONGREGATION: Yes!

L: Let's pray to thank God for giving us such good news, and for giving us feet to carry the good news to others. (*Prayer. Then allow time for children to get back into their socks and shoes.*)

A NEW THING (New Year)

Scripture: Isaiah 43:18-21
Focus: The focus of this sermon is that God is always doing a new thing in our lives. Part of our call as disciples is to become aware of what God is doing.
Experience: To reflect on the new things that may happen in our life in the coming year.
Arrangements: None are needed.

LEADER: Happy New Year to you all! Is everybody doing all right today?

CHILDREN: Yes!

L: Well, let me ask you a question: Were you different at the end of the year that just ended than you were at the beginning?

C: Yes.

L: So do you think you will be different at the end of this new year than you are right now?

C: Yes.

L: How will you be different? (*Children may remain silent.*) Well, stand up! Will you be taller?

C: Yes!

L: How much taller? Show me. (*Children indicate a wide variety of hoped-for growth.*) Great! Will you be older?

C: Yes!

L: How much older?

C: A year.

L: Just checking. And you did so well with that question that it's obvious you're going to be smarter, right?

C: Right!

L: And do you think you might have some new friends by the end of the year? Probably so! Look around: let's pick someone who we think might be our friend by the end of the year. Join hands with those friends. (*Children move around, joining hands—make sure everyone gets connected!*)

C: I'm going to have a new brother!

L: You are? I'm sure your parents will be excited to hear about that. (*This child's parents were "done" with their family and weren't expecting!*) What about you and Jesus? Do you think you'll learn some new things about Jesus in this new year? (*Nods*) And you may learn some new Bible stories by the end of this year that you don't know yet. Do you know about a man named Gideon?

C: No.

L: Do you know about the judge named Deborah?

C: No.

L: Do you know about the disciple named Fred?

C: There's no such thing!

L: Just checking. See, you're smarter already! Let's have a new prayer and thank God that we have so many new things to look forward to this coming year, as we keep following our Lord Jesus Christ into the future. (*Prayer.*)

TERROR AND AMAZEMENT (*Easter*)

Scripture: Mark 16:1-8

Focus: Flowing through the familiar story of Jesus' resurrection are the darker, more mysterious currents of the reactions of those who were actually there. In our efforts to joyfully proclaim the risen Lord, we sometimes overlook the mixture of emotions that were present in the actual event: anxiety mixed with astonishment, confusion mixed with celebration, worry mixed with wonder. In disregarding this mix of emotions, we may make the resurrection surreal, with seemingly little room for the natural reactions and questions of children. The focus of this sermon is on the terror and amazement of the women who discovered the empty tomb.

Experience: To walk to the tomb, to be surprised by the angel, to run back to a safe place, and to pray.

Arrangements: Check your "church geography" to verify where you will set the action around the "tomb." Many sanctuaries have a double door to the narthex that remains closed throughout worship, and this arrangement will work well. You will need an "angel" to be outside these doors, ready to throw the doors back and make his or her pronouncement. A costume, a flood light (a simple outdoor flood operated by an usher to back-light the angel), and a little rehearsal wouldn't hurt!

LEADER: The Lord is risen! What a special day this is: Easter! What happened on this day that makes us want to celebrate it so much?

CHILDREN: Jesus rose from the dead!

L: That's right. I thought this morning that we might pretend we are followers of Jesus who go to the tomb, or grave, and discover that he has risen. Let's get up and walk toward the back of the church. (*As you walk*) What do you suppose those women felt like as they went to Jesus' grave that morning?

C: Sad. Happy. Lonely.

L: I think that they might have been sad. They were going to be happy later, weren't they? But as they walked, like we are walking, getting closer and closer to the tomb, they were probably sad and lonely, and maybe a little scared. And the Bible says that they were also wondering who would roll away the stone from the grave. The grave was in the side of a hill, and a big stone covered its doorway—(*arriving at the "tomb"*) like these doors here. Let's all say that to each other: "Who will move the stone?"

C: Who will move the stone?

ANGEL: (*Cued by children's line to open doors dramatically— flood light turned on*) Do not be alarmed; you are looking for Jesus of Nazareth, who was crucified. He has been raised; he is not here. Look, there is the place they laid him. But go, tell his disciples and Peter that he is going ahead of you to Galilee; there you will see him, just as he told you. (*Light is turned off, doors close.*)

L: And do you know what the women did after they heard the angel say that? They ran away! (*Start running back toward the front of the church, to the usual meeting place of the children.*)

C: (*Should follow you; if not, call them as you run.*)

L: (*As you run*) The Bible says they were afraid and amazed! What do you say when you're scared? Aaaaaah!

C: AAAAAAH!

L: (*Arriving*) Let's pray! Dear Lord, help us to realize how scary it must have been for your disciples when at first they didn't understand that you were risen from the grave. Help us not to be afraid, as the angel said, and truly to celebrate your resurrection. Amen.

RUACH (*Pentecost*)

Scripture: Acts 2:1-13
Focus: This little word study is a fun way to focus on the meaning of *ruach*, the Hebrew word for Spirit, a word that also means wind, breath, and life. Through an understanding of this word, children should gain a better understanding of the power we receive from God's Spirit—the power that was shown on the first Pentecost.

Experience: To experiment with a "windy" pronunciation of various words related to the story of Pentecost and to discuss what happened when God's Spirit came upon the disciples.
Arrangements: None are needed.

LEADER: Good morning! Who can tell us what special day this is?

CHILDREN: Sunday? My aunt's birthday! Pentecost?

L: It's all those things, evidently, but it is especially Pentecost, a day that is a kind of birthday for the church. All Christian churches, everywhere, were born on a day fifty days after Easter when God's Spirit blew on the disciples like the sound of wind. What sound does the wind make?

C: Whooosh.

L: That's really good! Can you say the word "wind" in a windy way? (*You may need to demonstrate.*)

C: Whhhhhhiiiinnnd.

L: That works! OK, now try saying "breath" in a windy way.

C: Breeaaaathhhhh.

L: Good! How about "life"?

C: Llllliiiiiifffffe.

L: It's getting a little harder, isn't it? This one may be the hardest of all, how about the word "spirit"?

C: Ssssspppiiirrrrrriiitttt.

L: (*Pause.*) That didn't sound too windy, I'm afraid. But there's hope! Did you know that there's a word in another language, a language called Hebrew, that not only sounds windy, but means all the things we've been saying with all these other words? The word is *ruach*, and it means wind and breath and life and spirit. Can we say "ruach" in a windy way? (Ruach *is pronounced roo-ach, with the "ch" as in the Scottish word* loch.)

C: Roooooooooooaaaaaaaaawwwwk.

L: That was *really* good! And what does *ruach* mean?

C: Wind. Spirit. Life.

L: And breath.

C: Breath!

L: So when it says in the book of Acts that there was a sound like a rushing wind that came around the disciples, it is saying that there was a sound like what?

C: Whooosh.

L: (*Laughing*) All right, but also a sound like this: roooooaaaac-cchhh!

C: Roooooooaaaawwwk!

L: And when it says that the disciples were filled with the Holy Spirit, the book of Acts is telling us that they were filled with what?

C: Roooooooaaaawwwk!

L: Good! And what else were the disciples filled with? What does the word ruach mean?

C: Breath. Wind. Spirit. Life.

L: Right. And when the disciples were filled with God's Holy Spirit—with breath and life—they began to tell everyone else about where this wonderful life came from. They talked about God and about what Jesus had done and how much God loves everyone. And many people believed in Jesus and became his followers. Let's have a prayer to thank God for life and breath and wind and Spirit. (*Prayer.*)

SPEAKING THE TRUTH IN LOVE (*Father's Day*)

Scripture: Ephesians 4:15; 6:1-4
Focus: Intimate moments between father and child are sometimes few and far between. While this sermon, for logistical reasons, does not link fathers with their biological children (one father may have more than one child present, some fathers may not have any children present), it does focus on an intimate moment in which all fathers and children can speak to one another's hearts.
Experience: To connect fathers with children (some young, some old) and let these pairs "tell the truth in love to one another" by simultaneously repeating words from a baptismal liturgy (or passage of your choice).
Arrangements: None are needed.

LEADER: Will all the *fathers* please come forward? (*Make sure you get* all *the fathers, not just those whose children usually come forward for the children's sermon.*)

CHILDREN: Hey! That's not right!

L: Fathers, let me ask you a question. Which is easier: to tell the truth to your children or to tell almost the truth?

FATHER: Do you want the truth, or almost the truth?

L: (*Laughing.*) Well, all of you being good fathers probably will say that it is usually easier to tell the truth. And while it may not *always* be easier, we know it's always right. What I'd like for you to do now is to go find a child—not your own—and then await further instruction. (*Fathers go off to find children. It is likely that there will be more fathers than children. If that is the case, remind the fathers that everyone in church is a child: in other words, they can find another adult!*)

What I would like you to do now is to look one another straight in the eye, and each of you repeat after me, speaking directly to each other. Here we go (*speak the passage phrase by phrase, allowing time for each person in the pairs to repeat*):

> Child of God,
>> for you Jesus Christ has come, has struggled and suffered;
>> for you he has gone through the agony of Gethsemane
>>> and the darkness of Calvary;
>> for you he cried out ''It is accomplished,''
>> for you he triumphed over death . . .
> Yes for you he did all this, before ever you knew of it,
>> and so it is that we love God,
>>> because God first loved us.

Let's have a prayer to thank God for this special time together and to ask God's help as we look one another in the eye and speak the truth in love. (*Prayer.*)

WE ARE THE BRANCHES (*Homecoming Sunday*)

Scripture: John 14:15-24; 15:1-12
Focus: Studies show that more than seventy-five percent of people who come to church do so at the invitation of others. The focus of this sermon is to remind us of that fact, to remember who invited

each one of us, and to encourage us to keep the "branch" growing in the "vine of Jesus Christ."

Experience: To make a "branch" of the children and others in the congregation, tracing the invitational connections that brought them all into the church, and if possible showing the "fruit" borne of children (or their families)—the people whom they have in turn invited.

Arrangements: Have on hand a simple cross (representing Jesus) that will be at the center of the "vines," the lines of children and adults radiating out from it. You may also want to give some thought to the children normally present for a children's sermon and how they came to be part of the church.

LEADER: Good to see everyone today. I have a question for you: Why are you here? What I mean is, who brought you to church?

CHILDREN: My parents.

L: But who told them about the church so they would know to bring you? Let's ask them and find out. Amanda, stand up. Did your parents bring you to church today?

AMANDA: Yes. (*Nods.*)

L: Let's have them come forward. (*After parents arrive*) And how did you find out about the church?

PARENTS: From our friends the Benefields.

L: And the Benefields are here today, so let's ask them to join us. While they're coming, you join hands with Amanda and start to make a vine, or a branch off in that direction. Benefields, you join this branch. (*They join hands with Amanda's parents.*) Do you remember how you started coming here?

BENEFIELDS: My sister's minister called you and gave you our name, and you called us.

L: I remember that! So we need someone to stand at the head of this branch to take the part of that other minister. (*Find child or close-at-hand adult from congregation.*) Good! (*Now address another child.*) Christopher, stand up and tell me, did your parents bring you today?

CHRISTOPHER: Yes.

L: So let's have them come up here, and tell us how they came to know about the church. (*Wait for Christopher's parents to arrive.*)

PARENTS: Our minister where we used to live called and found out about it and told us.

L: Well, she's not here, so how about you (*indicate another adult in congregation*) coming up here to represent that minister? Now all of you—Christopher, your parents, and this substitute minister—hold hands and make a branch growing off in that direction. (*Now address a brother and sister among the children.*) Josh and Audra, will you stand up and tell us how you came to be here today?

J & A: Our mom brought us.

L: Teresa, will you come up here and tell us how you came to know about the church?

TERESA: You called us.

L: Yes, I did. And as I recall, I got your name from your mother, who is a member at another church but wanted you to know about this church. Let's see, will you (*indicate another adult*) stand to be Teresa's mother? (*Help family make another "branch" radiating out in another direction.*) Great! (*Address a new child in the group.*) Last one for today. I'm sorry I don't know your name.

NATHAN: Nathan.

L: Nathan, it's good to have you with us today. Would you be willing to stand up and tell us who brought you?

NATHAN: (*Shakes head.*)

L: Well, that's all right. I imagine your mom or dad brought you. Would one of them be willing to come up here? (*Parent comes.*) How did you come to be with us in worship today?

NATHAN'S PARENT: Our friend Jan invited us.

L: That's super. Jan, will you come up here, too? (*Help these people form the fourth "branch" leading out from the cross. Then address the congregation.*) You know, all of us probably have been invited to church by someone, and I hope that all of us have invited someone else in turn. So let's all stand up and join hands in one last long branch. All of you there at the center, hold on to the cross to remind us that it is Jesus Christ who is at the center of our "vine." Let's celebrate in prayer the work of being an evangel, sharing the good news of Jesus Christ with one another. (*Prayer.*)

THANK-YOU NOTES TO GOD
(Thanksgiving or Stewardship)

Scripture: 2 Corinthians 9:10-15
Focus: We have much to be thankful for, and giving thanks is the root of worship. The focus of this sermon is on giving thanks.
Experience: To write a thank-you note to God.
Arrangements: You will need a supply of pencils and thank-you notes. Store-bought notes can be adapted, but many churches or their members have computer software that can generate an affordable alternative.

LEADER: Would the children please come forward and bring an adult with them? I'm so thankful to see you all today! I wonder, What are *you* thankful for?

CHILDREN: My mommy and daddy. Jesus. My dog.

L: Those are all good things to be thankful about. Who are you thankful to?

C: God. Jesus.

L: That's right, and to help us say thanks I brought some thank-you cards and pencils. (*Distribute supplies to children.*) As you can see, on the cover it says, "Thank You God," and on the inside it says, "For . . ." and then there is space for you to write down one or two things you are thankful for. If you need help writing, tell the adult who is with you what you are thankful for and they can write it down, or you can draw a picture. (*Pause for time to write.*)

(*Collect pencils.*) During the offering, you might want to put your thank-you notes in the offering plate. (*Or you could collect these now in an offering plate.*) Let's have a prayer to thank God that we have so much to thank God for! (*Prayer.*)

STEWARDSHIP

HERE I AM

Scripture: Genesis 22:1; Exodus 3:4; Luke 1:38; Acts 9:10

Focus: The call of God comes to each person in a unique way, yet the experience of that call is universal to our Christian journey. The focus of this sermon is to explore the idea that God does call us to service.

Experience: To have each child hear his or her name called; respond as did Abraham, Moses, Mary, and Ananias, with the words "Here I am"; and receive a call to service.

Arrangements: You will need to know the names of the children who will be coming forward for the sermon (except for visitors, whose names you can ask) and have a list of "tasks" for them to carry out. (You can use the same task for more than one child.)

LEADER: Good morning! It's so good to see all of you today. I'd like to read you four verses from four different Bible stories about four different people. See if you can hear the one thing that is the same in each verse. Are you ready?

CHILDREN: Yes!

L: Here's the first story verse: "After these things God tested Abraham. He said to him, 'Abraham!' And he said, 'Here I am' " (Genesis 22:1).

Here's the second: "When the LORD saw that he had turned aside to see, God called to him out of the bush, 'Moses, Moses!' And he said, 'Here I am' " (Exodus 3:4).

The third: "Then Mary said, 'Here am I, the servant of the Lord; let it be with me according to your word.' Then the angel departed from her" (Luke 1:38).

And the fourth: Now there was a disciple in Damascus named Ananias. The Lord said to him in a vision, 'Ananias.' He answered, 'Here I am, Lord' " (Acts 9:10).

Did you hear one phrase that all four of the people in these stories said?

C: Here I am. I hear you. I am here.

L: Yes, I think it was "Here I am." God called to each of these four people—to Abraham, Moses, Mary, and Ananias—and God asked each of them to do something pretty big, even kind of overwhelming. But all of them said they would do it by answering, "Here I am." Does God call on us to do things, too?

C: Yes. No. Sometimes.

L: I think God does call on us, and we need to decide how to respond. How about if I call each one of you by name and ask you to do a task. If you agree to do it, you say: "Here I am." Got it? Laura, will you clean up your room this week without being asked?

LAURA: Here I am.

L: Becky, will you be nice to your brother today?

BECKY: Here I am.

L: Brian, will you give a dime this week to someone who needs it?

BRIAN: Here I am.

L: Jessica, will you pray for hungry children this week?

JESSICA: Here I am.

L: Ian, will you pick up the bulletins left in pews after church today?

IAN: Here I am.

L: Peter, will you bring something next week for the food box in the narthex?

PETER: Here I am.

L: (*Continue until all children have had a chance to respond.*) That's wonderful. You know, when you do kind and helpful things like these, you are really doing them for God: You are serving God, just like Abraham and Moses and Mary and Ananias. Let's have a prayer to thank God that we are sometimes called to serve by helping others. (*Prayer.*)

LOSING A HUG TO GET ONE

Scripture: Luke 9:23-27
Focus: One of the mysteries of our Christian faith is the way giving results in getting. While the world tries to grab and hold on to as many possessions as it can, Jesus tells us that we need to *give* in order to receive.
Experience: To play a hugging game twice, each time with a different rule. In the first game, everyone (the whole congregation can play this game) is to try to get as many hugs as they can without giving any away. After a minute, the game results will be reviewed

and the rule of the game changed. The next rule will be to give away as many hugs as possible.

LEADER: Good morning, everyone! Let's play a game. The rule of the game is that we should all try to get as many hugs as possible without giving any hugs away. Congregation, you may stand and play this game, too. Remember: Try to get as many hugs as you can without giving any away. Ready, go!

CHILDREN: (*After a moment*) This isn't working! (*Another child hugs self.*)

L: It's not working? Hugging yourself might be the only way you'll get a hug this way! Wasn't that fun?

C: Nooo!

L: Well, maybe we should change the rules a little. This time try to *give away* as many hugs as possible. Remember, congregation, you're playing too. Ready, go!

L: (*After several minutes*) Which way of playing the game was better?

C: The second one.

L: Why?

C: 'Cause we got more hugs.

L: Let's have a prayer to thank God that we get so much love when we give away love. And let's ask God to help us give away lots of love. (*Prayer.*)

GOD BLESS YOU

Scripture: Luke 12:48b
Focus: The Bible makes clear that we have been blessed so that we can in turn bless others. The first step in this process is to recognize and give thanks for the blessings we receive; the second step is to pass those blessings on to others.
Experience: To list a number of our blessings and then to pass on some of those blessings to other people.
Arrangements: You may want to have a flip-chart and marker if you decide to make a list of the blessings the children mention.

LEADER: Good morning!

CHILDREN: Good morning!

L: Today we're going to talk about blessings, or gifts, that God gives us. How many of you have been blessed by God?

C: (*Some tentative raised hands.*) Me!

L: I wonder how many of our blessings we could list if we tried? What are some of your blessings?

C: We say a blessing every night at dinner.

L: Well, good. Let's see: The fact that you can say a blessing to God is a blessing (*Note "mealtime prayer" on flip-chart*), and the fact that you have a dinner to eat is a blessing, too, isn't it? (*Note "dinner."*)

C: We had chicken for dinner last night. We had pizza.

L: That's wonderful. I can tell we're in a kind of dinner–food mood this morning! How many of you live in a house or apartment?

C: I do! Me!

L: That's a blessing. God has blessed your family with a place to live. (*Note on flip-chart.*) Now, what are some other blessings in your life?

C: Clothes, TV, dog, toys, etc. (*Note these as children mention them. Be prepared to supply additional blessings when things slow down: parents/family, church, school, trees, flowers, birds.*)

L: Whew! That's quite a few blessings. We've been blessed a lot. Do you think we need to say or do anything about all the blessings we've been given? What would be a good response?

C: Thank God?

L: Give thanks to God. Absolutely. That's an important thing to do every day. But do you know what else? God wants us to use our blessings to bless other people, too. There is a verse in the Bible that says something like this: From everyone to whom much has been given, much will be required; and everyone who has been given many blessings will be asked to give even more blessings away (*Luke 12:48, paraphrase*). This verse says that we need to *give away* blessings. So let's do it. We listed ten blessings that we received. So why don't we pick eleven people and say "God bless you" to them—and maybe even give each of them a hug as well. Those are fine blessings to give away. (*Send children into congregation; help those who can't count that high!*)

L: That was wonderful, but I wonder if that's enough?

c: No! (*They head off to bless some more.*)

L: Wait a minute, children! We can bless people all through the week—not only in what we say, but in how we treat them in the things we do for them. And we can bless other people because we feel so good about the blessings God has given us. Let's have a prayer to thank God for our blessings, and for the wonderful job we have of blessing others. (*Prayer.*)

GRABBING PLENTY

Scripture: 2 Corinthians 9:6-8
Focus: One of the mysteries of the economy of God's household is that the more we give away the more we have. This message is used by Paul to encourage the Christians in Corinth to give out of the abundance given by God. As Christians we are encouraged to recognize our abundance and to give freely, rather than grabbing for more.
Experience: To be involved in a "penny grab" in order to get enough money to buy a box of candy. When that "money-making" tactic fails, have everyone share their abundance so that all benefit.
Arrangements: Fill a shallow bucket with about twenty pennies per each child—a minimum of $1.00. Fix the price of a box of candy to reflect the among of money in the bucket. If your group is larger than seven, you might have several buckets of pennies available. (Have the activity overseen by adult assistants so children don't squash each other.)

LEADER: How are we all doing today? Do you see what I have? (*Hold up bucket.*) It's a bucket of pennies. In a minute I'm going to put it down in the middle of our circle, and let each of you try to grab as many pennies as you can. Do you see what else I have? (*Hold up box of candy.*)

CHILDREN: A box of candy!

L: That's right. And this box of candy costs $1.00. If anyone can grab a dollar's worth of pennies, she or he will be able to buy this box of candy from me. Ready? (*Set bucket in center of circle and make sure all children are an equal distance from the bucket.*) GO!

C: (*Grab pennies. Be sure to monitor this activity closely, especially if you have small children present. It need not go on for more than about fifteen seconds.*)

L: OK, let's count out your pennies. Laura, it looks like you have about twenty cents. Brian, you got a lot, didn't you? Let's see, maybe about thirty cents there.

C: I only got eight cents.

L: Well, that's all right, because it doesn't look as if anybody else got enough to buy the candy. What if I told you there was only a dollar's worth of pennies (*more if you used more*) in the bucket to begin with? What would you have to do if you wanted to buy the candy that costs $1.00?

C: Get all the money.

L: Get all the money. Right. But if we all grab for the money again, all of us will get some, and no one will get it all. And nobody will be able to afford the candy. How else could we do this?

C: Share?

L: (*Or leader can prompt: "Could we share?"*) That's right, we could share all the pennies that each of us has. Then there would be enough to buy the box of candy, and we could all share that, too. Do you want to do that?

C: Yes! (*Children make transaction.*)

L: Let's have a prayer to thank God that when we share what we've got, there always seems to be enough for everybody to get what we need. (*Prayer.*)

HAVING PLENTY

Scripture: 2 Corinthians 9:6-15
Focus: A key insight into Christian stewardship comes from Paul's words to the Corinthian church about sharing their abundance. God has provided us with every blessing in abundance, so we will always have enough to share.

Experience: To make a decision about how much is enough for us, then to confront the decision about what to do when we have more than we need.

Arrangements: You will need three containers, the largest of which should be about the size of a cup, and more than enough wrapped candy (peppermints, kisses, etc.) to overflow that cup. If your group is large, you will need to use larger containers. Make sure there is considerably more than one piece of candy per child.

LEADER: I'm so glad to see you! We have some hard work to do today. I have three containers: this little one, this medium-sized one, and this large one. Which of these do you think will hold enough candy so you'll each get a piece?

CHILDREN: That one! (*They will probably choose the largest.*)

L: Well, it so happens that I brought some candy along. So let's see if you're right. (*Pour so much candy into large container that it overflows. Express surprise.*) My goodness, there's more candy than we can fit into our container. Hmmm. What should we do with the extra pieces?

C: Keep it! Eat it!

L: We could do that. But didn't you say that if I filled this container we'd have enough for each of you?

C: (*Reluctantly*) Yes.

L: Maybe we could share the extra candy with some of these people who have the courage to sit here in front of the church. What do you think? Here: take some of this overflow and share it with them. (*Children take candy and distribute it. When they return, distribute one piece of candy to each child and ask them to keep these in their pockets until church is over.*) Now you've each got your own piece of candy *and* you had the fun of giving away nice gifts to other people. Wasn't it great to have more than enough? One of the neat things about being a Christian is seeing how God gives us more than enough—more than we need—of things like food and clothes and toys and love and happiness. And then we can take some of those "extras" and share them with others. Let's have a prayer to thank God for giving us so much and for helping to share with others. (*Prayer.*)

A GIVING OF GIFTS

Scripture: Ephesians 4:11-16
Focus: The subject of spiritual gifts is one that many of us may not know or think much about. Many Christians—both adults and children—have had little help identifying the unique spiritual gifts God has given them. Yet Scripture proclaims that God has gifted the saints in order to build up the body of Christ; and we believe that all Christians—adults and children—are numbered among the saints. This sermon will focus on identifying the unique gifts of the children.
Experience: For each child to hear their parents describe a gift that is unique to that child.
Arrangements: Somewhere in the morning bulletin, possibly in the announcements, include the following note:

> "Parents, please note! The children's sermon today concerns the gifts we all have in the body of Christ. Please identify at least one gift you've observed in your child (compassion, sense of humor, creativity, playfulness, organization, thoughtfulness, sensitivity, joy, hopefulness— these are just a few) and be prepared to say what that gift is when you are called on. Thanks!"

Before the service begins, direct parents' attention to the bulletin note, but don't describe its content.

LEADER: It's great to see all of you today! Let me ask you a question: When do you give gifts?

CHILDREN: At Christmas. For birthdays.

L: What kind of gifts do you give?

C: (*Name the latest toys.*)

L: And how do you get the gifts you give? Where do they come from?

C: I go buy them. From my mommy.

L: Well, did you know you have special gifts with you all the time? Let me read what it says in a book of the Bible called Ephesians: "The gifts God gave were that some would be apostles, some prophets, some evangelists, some pastors and teachers, to equip the saints for the work of ministry, for building up the body of Christ . . .'' (Eph. 4:11-12). Those Bible verses are saying that God gives special gifts to Christians—to you and to all of us here as well. These special gifts are things that we're good at or ways we can help others. Do you know what special gifts God has given you?

C: No.

L: Well, sometimes we need to have other people help us see what our gifts are and show us how to use them well. I've asked each of your parents to think about what special gift God has given you. As I call your names, I'd like your parents to name your gift loud enough for us to hear. Here we go: Justin.

PARENT: Justin has a wonderful imagination.

L: Tommy.

P: Tommy is warm and friendly.

L: Lacy.

P: Lacy is really sensitive to how others feel.

L: Benjamin.

P: Benjamin has a wonderful sense of humor.

L: Emily.

P: Emily is very loving.

L: Laura.

P: Laura is always cheerful and joyful.

L: Ian.

P: Ian is really thoughtful.

L: Let's thank God for giving us wonderful gifts, and for giving us loving people who can help us discover what those gifts are and how to use them. (*Prayer.*)

THE GIFT OF TEACHING

Scripture: Ephesians 4:11-16
Focus: The focus of this sermon, like the previous one built on the Ephesians text, is the identification of God's gifts to us. In this sermon, however, the children will identify gifts that God has given to the adults.
Experience: To identify an adult whom a child would like to have as a teacher.
Arrangements: None are needed.

LEADER: Good morning! It's good to see you all. Let's talk a bit about your Sunday school teachers. I'm sure you all like your teachers. But tell me: *Why* do you like your teacher? What's special about her or him?

CHILDREN: She's nice. He tells us stories. She's a lot of fun.

L: Those are good reasons. Your teachers sound like really special people. I wonder, how many of you got to choose your teacher?

C: (*No raised hands.*)

L: That's what I figured. Well, today I'm going to give you a chance to choose someone you might like to have as a Sunday school teacher someday. Would you like that?

C: Yes!

L: It doesn't have to be the teacher you have now, and the person you pick may never end up teaching; but I'd like you to go out into the congregation and pick someone you think you'd like to have as a teacher someday and bring them back here. Pick someone you think looks interesting, or someone you especially look up to, or someone who you think is loving and caring—anyone who might be a teacher you'd like to have. (*After children have returned with "teachers"*) Do you children know the names of the teachers you picked? Do you future teachers know the names of the children who picked you? Take a minute and get acquainted. (*After a moment*) Let's have a prayer to thank God that there are so many people out there we'd like to learn from, and let's thank God that sometimes people see gifts in us that we might not know we had. (*Prayer.*)

TOPICS

WHAT SHALL SEPARATE US? (Hope)

Scripture: Romans 8:38-39

Focus: Throughout our lives, we will encounter people, experiences, fears, ambitions, and temptations that seem bent on separating us from God. St. Paul is convinced that God's love in Jesus is stronger than all of these; he reassures us that nothing can separate us from God's love.

Experience: Various adult helpers will role-play the things in Paul's list, each one in turn trying—and failing—to take children away from the cross or other representation of Jesus.

Arrangements: You will need to choose some representation of Jesus, such as a cross or the communion table. You will also need to enlist and brief ten adults (a Bible class?) who will act out one of the words from Paul's letter (see list and suggestions below) and make an unsuccessful effort to "grab" one of the children away from the cross or communion table. The words and possible actions are:

death	hands crossed over chest in classic death pose
life	jumping up and down in a kind of celebration dance
angel	hands folded in prayerful attitude
ruler	royal bearing, hand as if holding scepter
present	pointing down, as if saying "here and now"
future	pointing away, as if saying "down the road"
power	flexing muscles in classic pose
height	hand up, as if measuring a tall person
depth	hand down, as if measuring a short person
anything else	arms out in sweeping gesture

LEADER: Would the children please meet me at the cross (by the communion table), and will my adult helpers please line up over here? (*Have the ten adults form a line around or parallel to children.*) What a great day, and how great to see you all! Do you know how much Jesus loves you?

CHILDREN: Yes. No.

L: That's a hard question to answer because Jesus loves us more than we can imagine. Jesus is determined to keep us close to him and not let anything in the whole world take us away from God—no matter how hard those things might try. A long time ago, a man named Paul wrote a letter to tell Christians how strong God's love for them was. I'd like for you children to hold hands here around the cross (communion table) while I read Paul's promise that nothing can take us away from God's love.

(*While you read, adults will pantomime things Paul mentions and try unsuccessfully to grab children.*) ''I am convinced that neither death (*pause for action and grab*), nor life (*pause*), nor angels (*pause*), nor rulers (*pause*), nor things present (*pause*), nor things to come (*pause*), nor powers (*pause*), nor height (*pause*), nor depth (*pause*), nor anything else in all creation (*pause*), will be able to separate us from the love of God in Christ Jesus our Lord. (*Invite the ten adults to step out of character and join hands with you and the children.*) Let's have a prayer to thank God for this wonderful, strong love of Jesus Christ! (*Prayer.*)

WHAT IS THE SHAPE OF YOUR FAMILY? (*Divorce*)

Scripture: Matthew 5:31-32
Focus: We live in a day when families are ravaged by divorce, and many good Christians are no longer in churches because of their feelings of guilt and failure. Into this brokenness the church is called to preach a word of grace, a word of love, and a word of hope. The focus of this sermon is that Jesus loves us, no matter what ''shape'' our family is in.
Experience: To use a series of geometric shapes drawn by the leader to discuss Jesus' love for the people in families of all shapes and sizes.
Arrangements: A flip-chart or large sheet of paper and a marker. During the sermon, you will draw the following shapes:

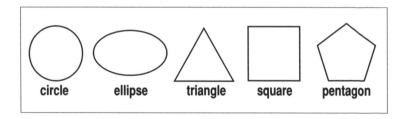

circle   ellipse   triangle   square   pentagon

LEADER: It's nice to see you on this great day, and I hope you're all doing fine. Gather around close. (*Set up flip-chart so children and adults can see.*) I'm going to draw a circle (*draw shape*), and we'll say that this circle represents a person. Does Jesus love us as persons, as single people?

CHILDREN: Yes.

L: That's right. And sometimes two people join together in marriage; so now I'm going to draw an ellipse—that's a shape like an egg—to represent those two people. (*Draw shape.*) Does Jesus love two people when they marry and make a family?

C: Yes.

L: Good. Now, sometimes, after two people are married, they add a third person to their family.

C: A baby?

L: That's right, they might have a baby. So we'll draw a triangle as the shape of that family. (*Draw shape.*) Does Jesus love this three-person family?

C: Yes.

L: And sometimes, if people are especially brave, they might have another baby. What shape is this? (*Draw square.*)

C: A square!

L: It's a square. And does Jesus love this four-person family?

C: Yes.

L: Right again. And I'm sure that some of you know families that have five people. (*Draw a pentagon.*) And some families have lots of children and even grandparents living with them. Do you think that Jesus loves all these kinds of families?

C: Yes.

L: But you know, sometimes two married people get separated and maybe even get divorced. (*Draw two separate circles.*) Then their family changes shape. Does Jesus still love the family—even though it's now a different shape? And does Jesus still love the two separate people?

C: Yes.

L: He sure does; he loves them very much. Jesus' love for us never changes—no matter what shape our families are. And he loves us whether we are married or single or divorced. Let's have a prayer to thank God for Jesus' love. (*Prayer.*)

FIRST AMONG YOU (*Leadership*)

Scripture: Matthew 20:25-28
Focus: Jesus reveals that the role of a true leader is that of a servant. The focus of this sermon is on servant leadership.
Experience: To take directions from two kinds of leaders and decide which kind of leader we like best.
Arrangements: You will need two adults to be leaders (you could be one). Brief these leaders beforehand on their roles and the instructions they are to give. (See below.)

LEADER: Hello! I have a question for you today. What does it mean to be a good leader?

CHILDREN: To be the boss. To be in charge. To give orders. To lead.

L: Those all sound like good answers, but I'm not sure we know yet what it means to be a *good* leader. Not to worry! We have brought here today, at great expense, two leaders with different leading styles. We're going to let each of them lead us and then decide which kind of leadership we like best. OK, Leader One, you begin.

LEADER 1: Everybody stand on one foot.

C: (*Stand on one foot.*)

L: (*Allow about a minute or long enough for children to grow uncomfortable and/or lose their balance.*) Leader Two's turn.

LEADER 2: I'd like everyone to stand still while I scratch your backs. (*After having scratched two or three backs*) Would those of you whose backs I've scratched help me finish scratching the rest of the group? Thanks so much.

L: (*When back scratching is finished*) That was good. Now it's Leader One's turn again.

L1: I want everyone to do a push-up.

C: (*Do push-up.*)

L: Good, good, now it's Leader Two's turn.

L2: I'm going to start rubbing shoulders. As soon as I've finished rubbing your shoulders, would you go and rub another person's shoulders? And as soon as that person gets a shoulder rub, would she or he please rub someone else's shoulders? We'll keep this up until everyone has gotten a shoulder rub.

L: (*When finished*) Well, thank you Leaders One and Two. Now I must ask the children: Which kind of leader do you like better?

C: Leader Two!

L: Why?

C: Because she was nicer! She did things for us. She made us feel good.

L: That's right: she led us by doing things for us, like Jesus did. Let's have a prayer to thank God for teaching us how to lead by serving others—just like Jesus did. (*Prayer.*)

WE'RE COUNTING ON HELPING (*Evangelism*)

Scripture: James 2:14-17
Focus: Evangelism is often understood to mean sharing the good news about Jesus through words alone. The text from James makes it clear that actions must also be part of faith sharing.
Experience: To see how many people aren't in our church by going outside to count cars, to imagine what those people might need, and to pray specifically for those needs.
Arrangements: Prepare two people in the sanctuary to lead the in-church dialogue while you are outside with the children. Then bring the children back into the sanctuary for the closing prayer. Also, you might ask a few ushers to help with the "traffic flow" of the children.

LEADER: Will all the children please meet me at the door? It's good to see you all today. (*Step out of church and allow children to gather just outside the church door, or where you can see the street.*) We're going to stand out here for a couple of minutes and count the cars that go by—there goes one now. Think about all the people who are out driving around instead of in church right now.

CHILDREN: There goes another one! That's two!

L: Here come two more. That's four cars already. And was there more than one person in some of those cars?

c: Yes. No. The first one had a bunch.

L: So we know that there are four—whoops, there's another one—*five* cars, and maybe as many as ten people who aren't in church right now.

c: There's another. That's six.

L: Good. Keep counting to yourself. And while you're counting, try to think of what some of those people might need—maybe the kinds of things they might be able to find right here in our church?

c: Food. Clothes. Bible study. Prayer. Jobs. Homes. Friends. Love.

L: That's a good list. Many of those are things that we have here, and we might be able to get some of the others—like food or clothes or jobs. How many cars have passed by now?

c: Ten. Eleven.

L: Wow, ten or eleven in just this short time? Well, let's go inside and pray for all those people and ask God to help us meet their needs. (*Lead children inside and invite the whole congregation to join you as you pray for the needs children have listed.*)

"IN-CHURCH" DIALOGUE:

ADULT 1: What are they doing out there?

ADULT 2: It looks like (or sounds like) they're counting cars.

A1: Hmmm. I wonder what that's all about.

ADULT 3: You know, I've wondered about all the people who drive by here on Sunday mornings. Most of them seem to be going somewhere other than church.

A2: I've wondered about that too!

A3: We have something really good here, but they just whiz right by.

A2: And you know that their lives are filled with all the same kinds of questions and needs that ours are. The challenge is how to reach them.

A1: It's sort of like being a missionary. There are so many opportunities, but you have to overcome the barriers. I guess we might be able to reach them by meeting their needs.

A2: You're right. That's what we should be doing as a church.

ROCKS AND FLOWERS (*Transformation*)

Scripture: Romans 12:1-2
Focus: Paul's challenging words to the Romans offer us a choice between conforming to the world and being transformed by our faith. This sermon explores both options.
Experience: To feel a growing physical pressure of congregation members around us while talking about ways in which we are taught to conform or pressured to act and think like others; then to burst through the rings of people by enacting the transformation of a bud to a flower.
Arrangements: Before beginning the sermon, explain to the adults that you'd like them to form rings around the children during your talk. As the sermon progresses, the rings will grow in number and close in tighter and tighter.

LEADER: Good morning! Let's all meet in the middle of the church. How many of you have ever played "Simon Says"? (*Motion to adults in surrounding pews to stand and form a circle around children. While you continue to talk, this circle will grow to be many layers thick as everyone in the church surrounds the children.*) Just about everyone! Well, then, you know it's a game in which you have to do what the leader says.

Another game like that is "Follow the Leader." (*Continue silently motioning to adults to stand and gather in around.*) In that game everyone does what the leader does. I bet sometimes you feel like other people are trying to make you do things, even when you're not playing a game. How many of you have ever got caught doing something wrong and told a parent that somebody made you do it?

CHILDREN: (*A few raised hands.*) Me! Not me!

L: Well, no one can really *make* us do anything, but sometimes we feel pressured. (*Motion to adults to move in tighter; they'll get the idea as they listen to you talk.*) We feel as if we're trapped, and the walls are closing in. TV ads make us feel that we have to get certain toys or act a certain way or dress in certain clothes. All of that is called pressure: people trying to make us think and believe what they want us to think and believe. (*By now you should all be pretty well packed in!*) All of that pressure can make us feel like a rock that's buried underground with tons and tons of weight crushing it on all sides.

In the Bible verses we read this morning, the apostle Paul calls this feeling being "conformed," and he tells us we shouldn't be conformed by doing bad things some people try to make us do. Instead, Paul says, we should be "transformed." What he means, I think, is that we should be changed—like a flower is changed from a bud into a bursting bloom. And Jesus can give us the power to change into people who do what God wants us to do— happy people. Wouldn't it be fun to be transformed like a flower and to burst into a bloom? Let's try it! Who is in the middle of all these people? Becky! How did you end up squashed in the middle? In a minute Becky is going to put her hands up in the air. And then all the people in the first circle around Becky, you put your hands up in the air, and maybe bend out a little bit. Then all the people in the next circle will do the same, and so on—kind of like the "wave" except that we're going to keep our hands up as we burst out from the center of our bud. Everybody ready? Becky, burst!

C: (*Becky thrusts hands up into air, the inner circle around her does the same and bends outward, and so on, until the entire congregation has burst forth like a flower. You may want to do this a couple of times, just for fun!*)

L: That was great! Let's all leave our hands up in the air and thank God that we don't have to conform to the pressures around us, but can instead burst forth, transformed into the kind of people God wants us to be. (*Prayer.*)

I REMEMBER (*Baptism*)

Scripture: Matthew 28:19
Focus: Martin Luther suggested that a key part of baptism is the daily and continual remembrance that God has claimed us as God's own. The focus of this sermon is to remind us of this claim any time we come into contact with water.
Experience: To connect words about remembering God's love with experiences that involve water.

Arrangements: Have on hand a pitcher of water and a glass. You will want to gather children near the baptismal font.

LEADER: (*Pour water from the pitcher into a glass and take a drink. Then put your hand on your head and say*) I remember Jesus loves me. (*Pause and look at the children.*) What just happened?

CHILDREN: (*Silence, shrugs.*)

L: Would it make more sense if I did this? (*Pour water from pitcher into the baptismal font, dip your hand in and sprinkle water on your head. Then say*) I remember Jesus loves me. (*Pause.*) What just happened that time?

C: You baptized yourself?

L: No. But I did feel the water on my head, and it reminded me that Jesus loves me. Here's why: The feel of water reminded me that I was baptized—when God claimed me as part of the Christian family. And so whenever I feel water, I remember how much Jesus loves me. When do *you* feel water—or get wet?

C: When I take a bath. When I brush my teeth. When I take my shower. When I get a drink from the water fountain at school. When I go to the beach.

L: I've got an idea! Every time you get wet or see water this week, put your hand on your head and say, "I remember Jesus loves me." Let's try it. Let's pretend you're taking a drink of water. (*Everyone pretends to drink.*) Now what do you do and say?

C: (*Put hands on their heads.*) I remember . . .

L: Jesus loves me.

C: Jesus loves me.

L: Good. Let's see: When you take a bath tomorrow morning, what will you do?

C: (*Hands on heads*) I remember Jesus loves me.

L: Great! And when you look out the window and see your neighbor watering the lawn, what will you do?

C: (*Hands on heads*) I remember Jesus loves me!

L: And if you're driving down the road and your mom or dad uses the sprayer to clean the windshield, what will you do?

C: (*Hands on heads*) I REMEMBER JESUS LOVES ME!

L: That's great. Let's hold hands and thank God that we have so many good reminders that Jesus loves us. (*Prayer. Before children get up to go, sprinkle a little water from your pitcher or baptismal font to test them!*)

THROUGH THE WATERS (*Baptism*)

Scripture: Matthew 3:13-17 (see also Matthew 1:18-24; 1 Peter 3:21-22; Mark 10:35-45; Colossians 2:11-12; Romans 6:8-11)
Focus: Baptism has a number of associations and connotations. The focus of this sermon is to touch briefly on a number of these associations: baptism as birth and rebirth, baptism as a washing or cleansing of our sin, baptism as a symbol for dying to sin, and baptism as a symbol of rising to new life with God.
Experience: A series of motions that enact and interpret some of the associations of baptism.
Arrangements: None are needed.

LEADER: Good morning! The story we read from the Bible today talks about the baptism of Jesus by John the Baptist. Jesus told John it was important for him to be baptized, and the Bible talks a lot about what Jesus' baptism meant. Today we're going to talk about what our baptisms mean. Everybody lie down on the floor and get into a little ball.

CHILDREN: (*Giggles as they scrunch up into balls.*)

L: That's it: pretend you're a little baby, waiting to be born. The Bible tells us that one of the things baptism means is that we are born again as children of God's family. OK, stand up now and pretend you are washing, as if you are taking a shower. The Bible also says that baptism means we are washed clean of all our sin and made ready to go to work for God. Is everybody clean?

C: Yes!

L: OK, now we need to pretend we're dead! Everybody lie down on the floor and act like you're dead.

C: I don't want to.

L: Well, that's OK. Will you sit down here with the rest of us?

c: OK. (*Rest of children lie down in "dead" poses.*)

L: It does sound a little scary, but the Bible says that when we're baptized we die to sin. In other words, we don't want to do bad things any more. I guess what we're really doing is burying the bad, sinful part of ourselves. Everyone had enough of being dead?

c: Yes! No!

L: Well, let's jump up, because baptism also means that we are going to rise from the dead just like Jesus did. What do you think Jesus looked like when he came back to life.

c: Shining. Alive. (*One child may raise his arms. If not, Leader can raise arms in triumphant pose.*)

L: Yes, all those things. Let's raise our arms real high—not just because we are rising from the dead, but because we want to praise King Jesus. Let's have a prayer of thanks for all of the things baptism means—especially for new life with Jesus. (*Prayer. Have a cheer after the prayer!*)

AFTERWORD

All of the preceding sermon models presume that children are present in worship. Yet, as Alan Smith suggests in his well-titled book, *Children Belong in Worship*, Sunday morning is often the most segregated time in America, not only in terms of black and white, but also in terms of child and adult.[2] In their book, *Engaging in Transcendence*, Barbara Kimes Myers and William R. Myers devote an entire chapter to children in worship, and they conclude with a section subtitled "Children Belong in Worship." They spend a major part of that chapter citing stories about children's participation in worship, and they do battle with the suggestion that children and adults be separated into two completely different worship experiences.[3]

Congregations that, for any length of time, have shipped their children off to the optimistically titled "children's church" know firsthand what Myers and Myers discovered from their overview of children's church institutions: "once out of worship, children rarely, if ever, returned."[4] Congregations must decide which concern is more important: a noise-free, adults-only worship service or the need to bring more youth into the church. Their decision will have a major impact on the growth of the church.

Children begin to understand the elements of language very early, long before they learn to speak. What they hear are the sounds, rhythms, and syntax that will later become the foundation for their communication. Children who are taken out of communal worship—or worse yet, never let in—will be cut off from the basic building blocks of Christian communion. The sounds and rhythm of the liturgy, the poetry of congregational affirmation, the heartfelt harmonies of our hymnody—all of these things are assimilated long before we know what to do with them. A child of three may not be able to sing a hymn, but it will become an underlying part of her faith experience when she hears it sung by the people of God around her.

There are two questions at issue in this matter. On the one hand, should we take children out of worship in order to train them for worship? The misguided logic of this question seems apparent as soon as it is voiced. No athlete misses a race in order to continue training. No actor forgoes a performance in order to continue rehearsing. No Christian adult stays away from worship in order to get ready to worship. The point is not *whether* we give children this kind of training in worship, it is *when*. Some time other than the congregational worship hour seems indicated, because this communal setting gives children an opportunity to put what they've learned into practice.

The second question is hinted at in the first, and is not quite so noble. Children can be distracting in worship: they wiggle and make noise and demand attention. Should we remove them from our worship service so the adults can be more comfortably attentive?

Before we answer that question, perhaps we need to rethink our baptismal vows. The church, as the *family* of God, is defined by its worship as a whole community—adults and children. I see the children's sermon as a way for adults to begin this rethinking, as they are welcomed to ''play'' and learn *with* the children.

As I came home from church the other evening, I saw a child of about six and a woman who was dressed in her business clothes, standing at the side of their house. Obviously just home from work, the mother had been invited by her daughter to play some kind of game. Both of them had their hands up in the air while the little girl jumped up and down. It was clear that the woman wanted to enter into her daughter's game as she made an attempt to jump—no small feat in hose and heels. I was struck by what the girl was offering her mother: a chance to step out of the seriousness and exhaustion of the adult world for a moment of childlike play. What a wonderful, welcome gift!

''Let the little children come to me, and do not stop them; for it is to such as these that the kingdom of God belongs. Truly I tell you, whoever does not receive the kingdom of God as a little child will never enter it'' (Luke 18:16-17).

NOTES

1. Sara Covin Juengst, *Sharing Faith with Children* (Louisville: Westminster/John Knox, 1994), 50–51.

2. W. Alan Smith, *Children Belong in Worship* (St. Louis: CBP Press, 1984), 14.

3. Barbara Kimes Myers and William R. Myers, *Engaging in Transcendence* (Cleveland: The Pilgrim Press, 1992), 11.

4. Ibid., 122.

Recitation in "Speaking the Truth in Love" was adapted from "Liturgy of Baptism, Eglise Reformée de France," as quoted in David S.M. Hamilton, *Through the Waters* (Edinburgh: T&T Clark, 1989), 128.

INDEX OF BIBLE PASSAGES

The number following each passage refers to the page of the children's sermon on which it occurs.